THE
positively
PRESENT
GUIDE TO *life*

THE positively PRESENT GUIDE TO life

dani dipirro

CREATOR OF POSITIVELYPRESENT.COM

WATKINS

Sharing Wisdom Since
1893

The Positively Present Guide to Life
Dani DiPirro

First published in the UK and USA in 2015 by
Watkins, an imprint of Watkins Media Limited
19 Cecil Court
London, WC2N 4HE

enquiries@watkinspublishing.co.uk

Managing Editor: Kelly Thompson
Senior Editor: Fiona Robertson
Art Director: Georgina Hewitt
Production: Uzma Taj

A CIP record for this book is available from the British Library

ISBN: 978-1-78028-999-1
ISBN (North America only): 978-1-78028-756-0

1 3 5 7 9 10 8 6 4 2

Typeset in Agenda
Printed in the United States

www.watkinspublishing.com

To anyone who has left a comment on my blog, written me an encouraging email or told me to keep writing — thank you. You are the inspiration for this book.

contents

before you
BEGIN

'm so glad you've picked up this book. Having it in your hands means you're thinking about living a more positively present life (or at least you're curious about what it means to do so), and that's awesome. Believe me, being more positive and more present is life-changing, soul-shaking, eye-opening, spirit-brightening stuff, and if you're ready to roll up your sleeves and do a little work, you're in for an amazing shift in the way you perceive and experience the world.

Before I get into all the good stuff – the tips, advice and inspiration for making your life as positive and present as possible – there are a few things I want you to know:

1   This is not a happiness book; while happiness is a great by-product of living a positively present life, happiness is not the end-goal here (you'll see why in the introduction).

2   You won't find PhD or any other fancy initials after my name; I know what I'm talking about not because I've studied in a classroom, but because I struggled for years with a negative attitude and I learned (often the hard way – through trial and error) how to live a more positive and present life.

3   While I can't guarantee everything in this book will work for you the way it's worked for me, I can guarantee that if you read this, do the exercises, and apply the techniques to your life, you will learn to live a more positive, more present life – a life that will ultimately make you happier, more fulfilled and more in love with every moment you experience.

Thank you for reading!

dani

INTRODUCTION

"Happiness is as a butterfly which, when pursued, is always just beyond your grasp, but which, if you will sit down quietly, may alight upon you."
American novelist Nathaniel Hawthorne (1804–1864)

Whether or not we choose to admit it, we all want to be happy. But how can we sit down quietly and enjoy happiness when we always have so much to do or so much stress to resolve? How can happiness find us when it's so easy to become distracted by the idea that we'll find happiness in the form of the latest "best" product, the newest health craze or the next fashion trend? The notion that we should actively pursue happiness is all around us – a never-ending parade of self-help books, online courses, and products "guaranteed" to make us happier. But if happiness is supposed to come via the *next* big thing, how are we supposed to be happy *now*?

The truth as far as I see it is we're not, or at least we're not supposed to be, happy in every single moment. To imagine that we can be *constantly* happy is to expect the impossible (and *always* being happy might actually be quite boring). Hawthorne was right: we shouldn't try to pursue happiness, but instead we should wonder at it when, like a butterfly, it alights on us from time to time. Don't despair at the thought that happiness might be fleeting, though. There's something worth striving for that can be even better than happiness. (Yes, even better than happiness!) And that is being what I call "positively present".

Before we look at what it means to be positively present, let's contemplate why happiness is temporary. Well, just as we feel angry or disappointed when things aren't going well, we feel happy when something goes right. In other words happiness is an emotion, a feeling that results from a particular trigger – a great meal, a loving embrace, a surprise promotion. It is not a perpetual state of being. Just as feelings of unhappiness (or anger or frustration) pass, so too do feelings of happiness.

ZERO IN ON THE BEST ASPECTS OF

now

Not recognizing the temporary nature of happiness has caused many people (including me) a great deal of *un*happiness. For years, I pursued the things I thought would make me happy – the newest gadget, the latest trend, the cutest guy. I experienced "happiness highs" each time I made a new purchase, enjoyed a delicious meal, or got the attention of a guy I liked. These highs were wonderful – filled with a rush of pleasure and the belief that, yes!, I was finally happy. But just like Hawthorne's butterfly, happiness would alight on me, fill me with moments of bliss – and then fly away again. Then I would once again go in search of (or wait impatiently for) another butterfly.

I continued this cycle for years, but on one snow-covered afternoon in February 2009, I realized something wasn't working and something had to change. I didn't want the rush of another night out, a shopping bag brimming with new purchases, or a midnight kiss from someone I'd shortly tire of. I didn't even want to rely on the more positive, yet still fleeting, happiness highs – an embrace from my mum, a belly laugh shared with a close friend, an afternoon with a great book, or a cuddle session with my dog. I wanted something that would last for more than a moment, but I also didn't have the patience to sit and wait, as Hawthorne advised, for a bit of bliss to land on me. In typical Generation Y fashion, I was sure I would find what I was looking for online in the magical, answer-filled world of the Internet. So, I sat cross-legged on my bed, laptop balanced on my knee in the middle of a chilly afternoon, scouring websites for a way to make happiness last.

After scrolling through page after page of happiness-boosting tips and tricks, I stumbled upon an article about "how to design an ideal life". An ideal life sounded great to me (who wouldn't want one of those?) and, after a quick skim, I saw that the exercises sounded easy yet soul-searching. Perfect for an impatient girl such as me. So I pulled out a notebook and got to work on the article's suggested exercises. The final exercise involved choosing two words from a longer list I'd been asked to make of all the things I wanted to experience in my life. My wish list was really long, including every single thing I wanted in life – from love and friendship to success and fulfilment to creativity and innovation to bliss and joy to inspiration and motivation. I took the process of narrowing down that list quite seriously. For a long time I perused it – and finally found and circled two words: positive and present.

It seemed to me that if I could learn to be "positive" – to see the good in every situation and find a way to make the most of whatever came my way – happiness, bliss and joy would naturally follow. And I was drawn to the word "present" because if I could stay present – focusing on what was happening now rather than what had happened in the past or might happen the future – I would worry less about what was already done, wonder less about what might or might never be, and instead find a way to make the most of my every moment, which would lead me to feel more successful, creative and fulfilled. The more I pondered the long list I'd created, the more I realized that, in some way, I could achieve each of the items on it if I could learn simply to be more positive and more present.

It was then that I had a great shift in how I thought about life. Instead of constantly trying to find happiness, which clearly hadn't been working for me, I decided I would try to be positive and present. As I read those two words circled on the page, I thought about creating some sort of mantra – a reminder for times when I found myself struggling to stay positive or present – and, after playing around with the words, I came up with the phrase "positively present". It was perfect. It represented what I had been longing to experience in my life – not a fleeting state of happiness I had to wait around for, but an active choice I could make every single day.

This was a major revelation for me. Being positively present was something I could do immediately, the fusing of two actions that I could perform at any time to create a life (not merely a moment) of contentment and acceptance. I didn't need specific things, people or situations to make it happen. All I needed was the moment and my mind.

The more I thought about my concept, the more it felt as if fireworks were going off in my mind and a big neon sign was lighting up with the word YES! You've probably heard of these moments – "aha! moments" as Oprah Winfrey would call them – when you finally realize what needs to happen and you suddenly possess strength and courage you didn't know you had to go after it. This was my moment.

I was so excited about my potentially life-changing realization that I didn't want to keep it to myself. I'd spent too much time on blogs and websites filled with advice and inspiration. It dawned on me that I, too, could create a website to share what I was experiencing and learning. Initially, I battled a bit of self-doubt. I'm not an expert on this, I thought to myself. I don't have a degree in psychology. I've struggled my whole life to be positive and present. What do I really have to offer in the way of advice? But with a little inner strength, I pushed those nagging doubts aside and set up a site, PositivelyPresent. com. I reasoned that maybe, if I eventually felt brave enough to share my words, I could help someone else learn to be positively present as well. It had been my lifelong dream to be a writer, and I'd been keeping a journal for as long as I could remember, so creating a site where I'd write about my daily experiences seemed to make sense. Even though I didn't know who would be reading my words, something in me knew I had to not only write down what I was experiencing and learning, but share what I'd written as well.

On PositivelyPresent.com I began documenting my journey of living a more positively present life. It started small, simply as a way to track my own experience and possibly engage other people – but it has since transformed every aspect of my life. And from the hundreds of emails, comments and letters I've received, it's had a big impact on the lives of others as well. Through the site, I connected with many who were feeling as I had – that the pursuit of happiness just wasn't working, that there had to be another way of looking at things – and the more positive feedback I received from readers, the more motivated and excited I became.

It was even more than a means to pursue a career as a writer; I had found my calling. I felt a deep, lasting contentment the first time I received an email from a Positively Present reader telling me how much I had impacted her life. Emails from men and women around the world started trickling into my inbox about how something I'd written had touched their lives – helped heal a broken heart, improved a friendship, transformed a mindset and, in one case, even prevented a suicide. While trying to make my own world a more positive and present one, I was also positively affecting the lives of others. And with the website in full swing, I felt all-the-more committed to staying positively present myself. Even when being so was difficult, I knew I had to try – not only for me, but for my readers as well.

Since I started the site in 2009, I've been surrounded by what brings me joy: I've found a way to build a creative, fulfilling writing career; I've curated my relationships, only keeping those that are positive; I've experienced deep, true love; and I've changed in many ways

... seeking the good in every situation and person (even when it's difficult to do so).

... staying in the present by refusing to dwell on the past.

... focusing on the now by not fretting about the future.

being
POSITIVELY
PRESENT
means...

... cultivating positive, productive relationships and avoiding negative influences.

... choosing to engage in activities and situations that bring out the best in you.

... coping with negative emotions, situations and people in a positive way.

– my attitude, my habits and my lifestyle. It's for these reasons that I've divided this book into the five sections of Home, Work, Relationships, Love and Change, which together cover every aspect of your life, from your physical environment to emotional and mental issues. Each of these areas of my life has been greatly improved by the choice to live positively in the present. And just as that online article helped me to find a way of life that works for me, I hope that my words – and the suggested exercises – will help you, too. You can either read through the sections in order or dip in where you feel you need the most help. If you want to declutter your home in order to declutter your mind, for example, start with Chapter One; if you're feeling overwhelmed by some of the relationships in your life, begin by taking a look at Chapter Four.

Why even write a book when I have the blog? Well, from the time I learned to write, I knew I wanted to spend my life doing it. I didn't always know exactly what I wanted to write about, but I knew I wanted to write books, because they have been my greatest teachers. I've learned so much about life – and about myself – from them, and writing a book is the best way I can think of to take the lessons I've learned from PositivelyPresent.com and explore them at a deeper level, compiling a guide filled with the insights I've come across since I created the site. And my blog has inspired this book in another way: all my advice here is presented in easy-to-follow lists, to make sure this guide is as simple to use and as practical as possible.

The aim of this book isn't to teach you the psychological, scientifically proven benefits of staying positive (of which there are many), nor is it to highlight the spiritual benefits of staying present (of which there are also many). Nor is the aim to show you how to be happy all the time (remember – that's not realistic), nor to show you the steps to take to make your life perfect (perfection really is the enemy of good). The aim of this book – much like the aim of PositivelyPresent.com – is to share with you what I've learned on my journey to becoming more positively present in my life, so you can try applying these lessons to your own life. My goal is also to show you why striving to be positively present – rather than pursuing happiness itself – has the power to be life-changing. Take a look at the diagram on the left to see just some of the ways to become more positively present in your life. Living according to these principles has helped me enormously – and now I hope it will help you, too.

THE POSITIVELY PRESENT PRINCIPLES

While writing this book I realized there are underlying principles that are relevant to all five chapters. Applying not only to the topics I cover specifically in this book, but also to life in general, I have called these six fundamentals the "Positively Present Principles" as they are the ones I have found most essential for living a more positively present life. Here they are:

principle #1
Open your mind to being positive and present.

principle #2
Be aware of – and willing to shift – your thoughts.

principle #3
Remove negativity whenever possible.

principle #4
Love and appreciate who you are.

principle #5
Adopt an attitude of gratitude.

principle #6
Focus on what inspires you.

Some of these principles might speak louder to you than others – and those are the ones you should tune into the most – but all of these, when put into action, increase the odds of you being able to make the most of every moment. Throughout the book I'll be coming back to these principles again and again, so take a look below to find more detail about why I think each one is so important. And don't worry if you aren't quite sure how the principles work in the real world yet. Once you start reading the rest of the book, all will become clear.

1. OPEN YOUR MIND TO BEING POSITIVE AND PRESENT

The first and most important aspect of living a positively present life is opening your mind to the idea of thinking positively in the present moment. Sounds simple, but when you're struggling through a difficult time in your life – or simply accustomed to embracing a negative attitude – positive thinking may not seem worthwhile, or even possible. Being willing to seek the good in the now doesn't mean being naïve about the presence of negativity or constantly existing in a state of blissful cheer; it means allowing yourself to let go of old habits (including old ways of thinking) and actively choosing to focus on the aspects of the moment that will help you create a more positive mindset.

2. BE AWARE OF – AND WILLING TO SHIFT – YOUR THOUGHTS

Your thoughts shape your world. When a situation appears to be good or bad, it is because you interpret it as good or bad. We use thoughts to label things, to try to make sense of them and to establish our moral code. Knowing a certain behaviour is unacceptable, or someone is a bad influence on you, for example, makes such moral judgments essential, but all too often, such labels can get in the way of the positive things in life, too. Amazingly, you can often change what you see by being aware of and willing to change the way you think about it. (It's kind of like magic!) Tuning in to your thoughts (rather than simply letting them happen) – an act that will take some practice if you're not used to it – allows you to see them for what they are and make a conscious choice to move them away from negativity and toward positivity. Likewise, you can redirect your attention from the past or the future to the present.

3. REMOVE NEGATIVITY WHENEVER POSSIBLE

Once you've made an effort to be aware of your thoughts, it's time to take a look at what's happening around you and how it affects your ability to live positively in the present moment. First, identify any negativity in your life. Consider your activities, habits and mindsets, as well as the people around you. What aspects of your life cause you to feel excessively unhappy, stressed, angry, nervous or unsettled? (Note the word "excessively". It's OK to feel these emotions in moderation, but when you feel them constantly or to a strong degree, something in your life is not good for you.) If you can, try to avoid – or at least limit your interactions with – negative influences to free up your life for more positive people and situations. Of course, it's not always possible to remove negativity completely (for example, you may not be able to entirely avoid the boss or mother-in-law who stresses you out), but it's usually possible to limit or reframe your interactions with them and it's always possible to limit the amount of time you give to thinking about negative situations or people.

4. LOVE AND APPRECIATE WHO YOU ARE

If you feel unhappy with who you are, it's very difficult to feel happy about the life you're living. Loving yourself (I call it "self-love") is about self-awareness – knowing and liking who you are, who you've been and who you want to be – but it's also about acceptance, which means loving not only the obviously lovable parts of yourself, but the parts that you might someday want to change, too). The second and equally essential aspect of self-love involves actively appreciating yourself. You can show appreciation for yourself through your words and actions, by telling yourself – every day, if possible – how valuable you are and how lucky you are to be you. You can also treat your body and mind with kindness – eating well, resting when you need to and allowing yourself to be who you are without too much judgment. In short, appreciation is love put into action.

5. ADOPT AN ATTITUDE OF GRATITUDE

Having an attitude of gratitude might sound clichéd – and even a bit silly – but it means paying attention to the things you have to be thankful for, rather than dwelling on what you feel you lack. When your mind is focused on the positives in your life, you're in the moment, appreciating what you have and who you are right now, in this moment, instead of worrying about what you wish you could have or longing for what you once had in the past. When you are thankful you are attuned not only to your own blessings, but also to those of the world around you, making it much easier to stay in the moment and appreciate the moment for all it contains.

6. FOCUS ON WHAT INSPIRES YOU

The moments you spend doing what fills you with joy and inspiration – like spending time with a loved one or engaging in a favourite hobby – are the moments in which it is easiest to be positively present. If you don't yet have something you love to do more than anything else, pepper your life with new experiences until you find what excites your heart and mind. When you find yourself lost in the moment, with no idea of the time and little desire to be anywhere other than where you are, you've found your activity, whether that's playing the guitar, painting a picture, spending time with your child or trekking up a mountain. What's inspiring and fulfilling may not always be straightforward (like raising children) or fun (like a job you love but find stressful), but anything that encourages you to embrace the moment is something you should make a priority in your life.

Throughout the book, you'll see reminder boxes that refer back to these six key principles. You'll also find "Apply It!" boxes, which give practical exercises that together make up a complete "positivity programme", helping you to take a positive approach to your home, work, relationships, love life and experience of change. If you give all these exercises a go, you'll be well on your way to living a positive and present life!

CHAPTER ONE

being positively present at home

hy is it so important to start this book here, with the home? Well, for a start the word "home" means so much more than the place where you live. The walls around you and the roof above your head make up your house (or apartment or room), but they are not your home. A "home" is far more meaningful, especially when it comes to creating a positively present life.

Your home – which might be a full-scale house, a tiny apartment or even just a bedroom – is your personal space, a reflection of who you are, who you've been and who you hope to be. If your home is filled with clutter, stress, negativity or unpleasantness, those negative aspects surround you every moment you're among them. How can your home become a place to breathe a sigh of relief – a place to exhale the pressures of the day, a refuge, a place to inspire you – if you walk through the door to face more stress?

It's important to make your home your positively present headquarters, where even cranky housemates (however they manifest – tantrumming toddlers, moody teenagers, argumentative siblings, stressed-out roommates, to name a few) can't upend your inner state of calm. There are tons of resources – whole books even! – dedicated to the task of creating peaceful home environments, but if you're anything like me, you need solutions you can implement quickly and simply. I mean, how in the world am I supposed to set aside an entire weekend for sorting through my closet? And who has the space for a meditation area?! As I've worked to create a more positive and present life for myself, I've come across many simple (and mostly cost-free) tactics that can transform a home from a place of clutter and stress to a space for inspiration and rest. In this chapter, I'll share my dwelling-related advice, from choosing décor that creates a positive living space to techniques that will help you be relaxed, tranquil and fully present at home, as well as cope with any difficult housemates. Tiny transformations at home can have a surprisingly big (and positive!) impact on the rest of your life.

living CREATING A POSITIVE *space*

Your living space can and does have a massive effect on how you feel. Objects, colours, patterns, scents and sounds all constantly influence you in some way. There are few places in life where you can make choices (even if they have to be collaborative with the other people you live with) about what you have around you, and your home is one of those magical environments. Before you go any further, think about what kind of living space you want to create. Are you looking for somewhere that inspires, excites and motivates you? Or, is your priority to create somewhere that calms, de-stresses and refreshes you? Perhaps you're looking to make a home that both relaxes *and* invigorates you? Whatever it is you long for, you have the power to create that space.

It would be unrealistic for me to tell you that your home is going to be a place of positivity every moment of every day. However, using the various elements that make up a home – furniture, colours, decorations and, of course, your relationship with the other people in it – you can create a space that makes it easier for you to nurture the good in your life and minimize the bad. I can't tell you what to put in your home. We are all wonderfully unique and we won't all have the same tastes (for example, you might hate the bright orange couch that I can't imagine my living room without), but I can share with you how I managed to make my living space (tiny as it is) more positive in a way that I hope you can apply to your own, uniquely "you" home.

1. INCORPORATE VISUAL INSPIRATION

What do you love to look at? What makes your heart sing when you see it? Think about the word "inspiration". What images does it conjure up in your mind? Perhaps you see pictures of your loved ones? Prints featuring words of wisdom? Snapshots of experiences you've had? Now think about how you can fill your home with these things.

home
IS WHERE
YOU FEEL LIKE
you

If words resonate with you, frame your favourite quotation and hang it where you'll see it every morning when you wake up. If a specific work of art sets your soul on fire, buy a print and display it so you will notice it when you walk through your front door. If images of your family fill your heart with joy, line your walls with photographs. And remember that, although your true emotional state lies within, what you see around you is likely to influence how you feel. If you want to feel excited and invigorated at home, choose vibrant and stimulating colours and items. If you prefer a relaxing, serene vibe, choose objects that evoke tranquillity.

2. CELEBRATE YOUR ACCOMPLISHMENTS

A positively present home should remind you how great you are. If you look closely at your life, you'll be surprised by all that you can be proud of. Perhaps you have been awarded a soccer trophy, a commendation in a music examination, a swimming badge, a promotion – or even an Olympic medal. Perhaps you took a photograph or painted a picture that beautifully captured a moment in time. Reminding yourself of your accomplishments throughout your home cultivates self-love on a daily basis. No one likes a show-off, so if you already have a case of trophies on display in your hallway, you've got it covered! But if you're like most people, you're probably not giving yourself enough credit for all you've done well. Instead of hiding your life's highlight reel by tucking away diplomas, awards or handmade art, put your trophies on a bookshelf (use them as bookends if you don't want it to seem obvious); hang your own photos or artwork in the living room; leave your journal of poems on the coffee table for all to read. Whatever you value or makes you feel good, show it off in your home. The more you remind yourself how awesome you are, the easier it will be to embrace the act of loving yourself.

reminder!
POSITIVELY PRESENT PRINCIPLE #4

Love and appreciate who you are by displaying your accomplishments and focusing on what you've done well, particularly when you're having a hard time staying positive.

3. CHOOSE YOUR COLOURS

Even if you're no interior designer, trust your instinct – you're bound to have an eye for colours that appeal to you. Think about which colours, whether calm, energized or full of imagination, evoke the emotional state you want to feel in each area of your home. It might be as simple as asking yourself what your favourite colour is. If you're like me, there might be one obvious answer (orange, always!), but if you have two or three favourite colours, there's no reason not to embrace each of them in some way. Take a look around your home. Can you see your favourite colour(s)? If so, great! If not, make changes! You don't need to open a can of paint (although that works); you can equally buy a throw, make a cushion cover, print off a picture, or display ornaments that showcase your favourite colours. Now, think beyond your favourites. Studies suggest that just looking at certain colours can evoke emotions and dramatically impact mood (for example, blues and greens are said to be calming tones; while reds are considered passionate and filled with energy). Look online to see what colours could trigger the emotions you want to experience in your home, and surround yourself with those.

4. STAY TRUE TO YOU

It can be tempting to see a home-décor style in a magazine and want to emulate it. But ask yourself, is that minimalist counter/ornately embroidered bedlinen/shocking pink couch really a reflection of who you are? It might look great in a photograph or in someone else's home, but how would *you* feel to live with it? Home décor is extremely personal. Unlike an office space or a shop layout, your home doesn't have to appeal to the masses. You're not trying to sell furniture (that's for catalogues) and you're not trying to showcase all of the latest trends (that's for magazines). What you're trying to do is to create a space that feels perfectly "you" – a space that helps you feel how *you* want to feel. The way your home is set up should be a reflection of your life and the way you live it. If the sofa suits you best sitting square in the middle of the room, put it there. If you're on the shorter side and you want your artwork to be at your eye level, hang it lower than the "experts" recommend. If you like gold *and* silver finishes, but read you should pick just one, incorporate both anyway. The more you design your home around what feels right for you, the more you'll enjoy and thrive in your living space.

5. TRY A TWEAK OR TWO

Creating a living space you love doesn't have to mean spending lots of money on new furniture or on a wholescale redecoration. Creating a positively present space is about taking what you have and making the most of it. Switching things up by making little changes here and there can be one of the best ways to get in touch with what works best for you. Sometimes you need to make only the tiniest of tweaks to revitalize your living space and feel more in tune with it. For example, think about how one small change could influence how you interact with, or move around, your home: perhaps you're always catching your knee on an awkwardly placed chair, so you move it to avoid bumping into it. It's amazing how little it takes to refresh your space – for example, try hanging a picture on a different wall, rearrange the furniture in your living room or bedroom, or change art for photographs of family. Even tiny tweaks can make you feel as if you've just moved in.

6. KNOW IT'S NOT FOR EVER

Over the years, you – and your home – will change. The colour you love on the walls in your bedroom right now might one day seem dreary or too much like the you of yesteryear. The paintings you hang on the walls with excitement today might at some point in the future seem boring and drab. When you choose soft furnishings, colours, artwork and so on for your home, know that they don't have to be with you for ever – and that's OK. The idea of for ever can be daunting – sometimes even paralyzing, which is why it's important to focus on what's happening in the present moment. If today feels like the day to paint a wall in your bedroom bright blue, do it! Don't let the idea of for ever stand in your way. Stay in the moment and surround yourself with the colours, styles and furnishings that appeal to you now. Surround yourself with the things that inspire, excite, relax and revitalize you right now, in this moment.

APPLY IT!
assess what works for you

Creating a positively present living space starts with figuring out exactly what makes you want to stay positive and present. Things that inspire and excite you – your favourite things – are what you want to have all around in your home. Grab a pen and answer the questions below, then use the answers to help you identify how to make your home the most positively present space possible. Don't want to write in this book or want to share this exercise with your housemates? Visit danidipirro.com/books/guide for a free, downloadable worksheet.

• My favourite colours are ...

• Books/magazines I enjoy are ...

• I like to collect ...

• Artwork that inspires me includes ...

• I feel most at home when ...

• Architecture I'm drawn to is ...

• Music I listen to at home is ...

• My favourite season is ...

• My dream home would include ...

DECLUTTERING
TO CLEAR *mental stress*

Clutter can be a source of negativity in so many homes, which is why I've dedicated an entire section of this book to it. However, I also believe clutter is relative. A pile of last year's birthday cards you might see as clutter, I might think of as a heap of treasured memories; you, on the other hand, might think it's useful to collect odd socks in case of finding the other in the pair, whereas for me they are straight for the bin. Clutter is a matter of opinion, but when you don't feel settled in your space, when you constantly feel as if things are messy or need to be put away, and when what's around you becomes a source of internal unrest, you've reached your personal clutter threshold.

As dramatic as it sounds, I believe clutter gets in the way of living. How can you feel relaxed and at peace in your home when clutter prevents you from staying in the moment and makes it so much harder to be positive? Here is my list of decluttering benefits. Removing clutter ...

- ... saves time (no more looking for a stray glove or missing keys);
- ... saves money (no more buying yet more sunglasses because you can't find your original pair);
- ... saves space (no need to ram things into drawers or cupboards); and
- ... saves your sanity (no more wondering why you're always losing things).

As you clear space in your home, you clear space in your mind. The tricky part is, of course, actually doing the clearing. First, don't listen to the voice telling you you don't have time for decluttering. Look at that list of four decluttering benefits – how can you not have time for them? They are essential to your ability to remain positively present at home. Here are my practical tips for decluttering your home.

1. IF YOU DON'T NEED IT, GET RID OF IT

Start with just one cupboard or drawer (make it one that irritates you every time you open it). Take out everything in it. Focus your attention on the present. Instead of thinking "Someday I might need this ..." or "I used to use this for ...", consider whether or not you need or use it *now*. Once you decide an item isn't necessary now, don't wait to give it away or throw it out – put it in a charity store bag (or the bin if it's no use to anyone else) straightaway. Here is a quick-reference flowchart that summarizes this process.

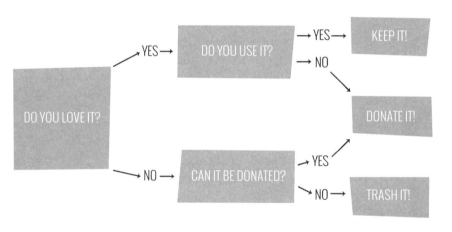

Be ruthless and don't ponder – follow your instinct. If you haven't used it (or even looked at it) for more than three months, you don't need it now. (Of course, there's always the possibility that you might one day wish you still had it, but based on my experience, you won't lament the loss for long.)

Now that you've done this with one cupboard or drawer, extend the principle throughout your home. Stop walking past unused or unwanted items; pick them up and throw or give them away. If you don't need it, don't use it and don't love it (and, no, you *do not* love those beaten up old boots of yours that you haven't worn this century), get rid of it. Not only does this removing excess stuff clear away clutter, it also allows the things in your home that you *do* cherish to step out from beneath the shadows. These are the truly beautiful, meaningful or useful things you wouldn't feel quite at home without. Remember: your home is not defined by the number of things in it, but by the feelings those things evoke in you. If you allow your positive possessions to shine, your home will be a happier and more tranquil place for you.

2. TAKE AN INVENTORY OF EVERYTHING YOU OWN

As you get rid of the items you no longer need or want, gradually assess what you have left. If you're a list-maker, make a list of the items you own. If lists aren't your thing, take photos on your phone, draw pictures, keep a mental diagram – do whatever works for you. As your inventory builds up, you'll start to notice duplicates – triplicates even – of more stuff you don't really need. (The first time I did this, I discovered I had 15 bikinis. 15! Out went most of them, along with a whole heap of mental clutter. The bonus was an extra drawer of space!) Taking an inventory is also a great way to keep in check what you'll need in the future (I know better than to buy a new bikini) and to remind you of all you own and should be grateful for. The next time you find yourself standing at your closet door about to mutter, "Ugh. I have nothing to wear!" check out your inventory, then pick something on it to wear and be thankful!

reminder!
POSITIVELY PRESENT PRINCIPLE #5

You can adopt an attitude of gratitude by creating an inventory of what you own. Being grateful will make you less likely to focus on what you lack, making it easier to stay in the moment and appreciate what you already have.

3. INVEST IN QUALITY ORGANIZING TOOLS (AND USE THEM)

When you start getting organized and getting rid of what you no longer need, you might think now's the time to buy things – boxes, bins, label makers, files, to name a few – to help you organize better what you have left. Believe me, I love those things, but don't let yourself get carried away just yet. As exciting as it is to be organizing your space (or am I the only one who gets excited about organizing?), it's usually a mistake to run out and buy tons of organizing items you may or may not need. Look back at your inventory.

set free
WHAT YOU NO
LONGER NEED

With it right beside you, look online at the organizational options. What boxes, folders, files and so on best suit your needs? Make a list. Finally, head out to a store and purchase *only* the items on your list. If possible, invest in high-quality materials likely to survive moving house, rambunctious children, curious pets and any other destructive forces you may have at home. Remember: first assess, *then* invest. And keep your receipts. If you don't find yourself using a specific organizing tool right away, return it for something you will use. Nothing undoes your organizing efforts like accumulating more clutter!

4. START COLOUR-CODING

OK, so you've surrounded yourself in your favourite, most uplifting colours. They are on your walls and in your soft furnishings. Now it's time to look at how colour-coding can help you declutter. For example, you can use colour to denote categories in your filing system. Assign a specific file colour to each area of your life (health, work, kids, car and so on), to make it easier to find exactly what you're looking for when you open your filing system. Let's say you use a blue section in your filing for anything related to your car. When your insurance comes up for renewal, you won't need to remember that you've filed the papers under "car", rather than, say, "Honda" or "insurance", because everything to do with the car is in the blue folder. If you have children, you could try colour-coding their drawers to encourage them to help put away their own clean laundry – "T-shirts go in the red drawer." Then, in the morning when it's time to get dressed, they'll know where to find their own clothes, too! Although it might take a bit of effort to set up a colour-coding system, in the long run you'll save lots of time you might have spent searching – giving you back more moments to enjoy.

5. KEEP THINGS IN LOGICAL PLACES

Seems obvious, right? Not always. Take a look at your kitchen, for example. Do you have all the things together that should be together? Is your coffee near the coffee pot? Is your tea near the teacups? Think about how you use your space and the things in it, and make it all as accessible as possible. The best way to start your assessment is to focus on being in the moment. Think about what you're doing while you're doing it. Do you move easily from one element of a task to another, seamlessly finding what you need? Or, do you find yourself getting irritated as you reach for or search for things? Does a task seem

APPLY IT!

tackle the junk drawer

If you're anything like me, junk drawers (and closets ... and rooms ...) are likely to make you cringe every time you open them. Worse than that, though, they provide a hiding place for all the things you don't really know what to do with – and that only encourages disorder. So it's time to get rid of that junk drawer once and for all!

Purging the junk drawer:

1 Empty the drawer on to a clear surface.

2 Place items in one of three categories: (1) Trash; (2) Donate; (3) Keep.

3 Throw away the "Trash" pile immediately.

4 Put the "Donate" items by the door so you can give them a new home.

5 Determine whether or not you really need the "Keep" items.

- If you do, sort them into categories, then arrange them in small boxes in the drawer.

- If you don't, add them to the "Donate" pile.

- If you're still not sure, pack them in a box and store it away, then mark a date on your calendar to check the box in a few months. If you haven't needed or thought about the items in all that time, donate them.

disjointed and unnatural? When you feel irritated or like you're faltering, consider how you might reorganize your space so everything is in the best, most useful place.

6. MASTER THE ART OF THE TO-DO LIST

I know – if you're "less-than-organized" (sounds better than "disorganized", right?) the mere thought of making a to-do list might make you shudder with irritation. However, no matter how much of a pain it seems to make one, a to-do list works. When you write down what you need to get done over the course of the following hours, or even week, you relieve your brain of the stress of focusing on the *next* thing, rather than on what you are doing now. Regularly writing down what you need to achieve, and then ticking items off as you do them, clears away the mental clutter so you can become much more at peace in the present.

7. PUT EVERYTHING AWAY STRAIGHTAWAY

Do you walk through the door and drop your purse on the hallway floor? Do you put mail on the side as soon as it drops through the letterbox, then let it stack up? Did you take out the camera charger and then leave it plugged in even once you'd finished charging the battery? One of the key things you can do to decrease clutter in your life is put things away *straightaway*. Once you've created a place for everything, keeping things clutter-free comes down to one basic (but often hard-to-follow) piece of advice: *put it away*. If you've organized everything but then don't put things back in their designated places, all the time you've spent organizing has been wasted. And no one wants to waste time, right? While you're putting everything away, also try to assess whether where you put things still works for you. If you find it's difficult to reach the bin of scarves on the top shelf in your closet (making it much easier to leave your scarves lying around in your room instead), move that bin so it's more easily accessible. As for the mail – open it, read it, then file it or discard it. Straightaway. No more piles of paper and scruffy open envelopes will equal a more positive, peaceful home.

MAKING THE MOST OF
at-home moments

When I get home, I like to kick back and relax in my own space and enjoy some time away from the stress of the outside world. Sounds easy, right? But wait. There's a pile of laundry, the lawn to mow, the recycling to sort out, the supper to cook, the bills to pay ... Sounds familiar? In this section I'm going to share my advice for minimizing the time spent on the business of household management, so you can really make the most of *enjoying* your home. I've discovered that if you find creative, efficient ways of doing what needs to be accomplished (the sort of approach you might take to your work in the office), all of those pesky little tasks can get done more quickly, leaving you with more free time at home. And more free time means more time to do the things you love (sitting down with a good book, being creative, listening to music ...), allowing you to feel more positive – and present in each moment – in your private space.

1. PUT OFF PROCRASTINATION

Remember your to-do list? The best day to check things off is today. After all, you really never know what tomorrow will bring. If you can complete a task quickly and easily, do it as soon as you can so you don't have to think about it any longer. If you can't complete the task in full right away, break it down into smaller steps and resolve to tackle each step one day (or week) at a time. For example, let's say you're struggling to cross "Organize kitchen cabinets" off your to-do list. If you have a whole day to dedicate to the task, schedule it on your calendar just as you would an appointment or event – and don't let yourself back out of it. If you don't have the opportunity to tackle it all at once (one of the reasons most of us put off tasks), divide it up into manageable chunks (perhaps one cabinet at a time; or the baking paraphernalia one day and the crockery the next; or in half-hour slots) and schedule those. The more manageable you make the overall goal, the more likely you'll be to put off procrastination and actually get to work.

DO YOU *really* NEED TO DO IT?

2. PRIORITIZE YOUR LIST

Sometimes items get added to a to-do list because you think you *should* do them – or think you should *want* to do them. On closer review, however, you might realize some tasks aren't as vital as you thought they were. Consider each task or chore with its purpose in mind. Do you *really* need to do it? How does it help to make your life more positive and/or present? Now, prioritize your list, focusing on the essentials and leaving the "should dos" rather than the "need tos" for another time. You've promised a dessert at a dinner party? Take fruit; or buy a dessert rather than making it. For the things that really do need doing (the laundry, for example), set yourself a time limit or a goal – two loads by lunchtime, say – and treat yourself to some me-time while the wash cycle is on. (What about the putting away? Make piles for everyone in your household and let them share the burden!)

3. USE TECHNOLOGY WISELY

In the home, technology can be both a blessing and a curse. On the one hand, it provides connectivity with loved ones, entertainment and instant information. On the other, it can become a distraction, a time-waster or a cause of stress (24-hour access to email is great until you open the one work email it would have been better to know about – and deal with – when you were in the office). Balance is key. Set limits for yourself. For example, turn off your email app on your smartphone at a given time in the evening or at the weekends. Try limiting yourself to an hour or two of TV a night; instead, read a book or play a game with a housemate, talk, enjoy each other's company! If you can, close down all electronic devices an hour or two before you go to bed; you'll sleep better – I promise.

reminder!
POSITIVELY PRESENT PRINCIPLE #2

Be willing to shift your thoughts by embracing the idea that doing one thing at a time will allow you to stay more present and more productive all day long. It may seem hard to believe, but multi-tasking really isn't the best way to get things done at home!

4. AVOID MULTI-TASKING

I know, multi-tasking is something everyone wants to be good at and now I'm suggesting you avoid it! Although it might seem counterintuitive, one of the best ways to get lots done is to do just one thing at a time. When you give your full attention to a single thing, with all your energy dedicated to the act of getting it done, you're more likely to complete it to the best of your ability (so you won't have to do it again or make any corrections later). Doing one thing at a time also encourages you to stay fully present and engaged in the moment, which is exactly what being positively present is about.

5. ASK FOR HELP

We can all use a little help every now and then. When your to-do list starts to feel overwhelming, review your tasks to see if you might be able to outsource anything. Instead of preparing a fancy meal for a party, for example, ask friends to bring their favourite dishes. Don't be afraid to delegate. You don't have to do it all yourself. The more you can pass off to others, the more you can focus on tasks only you can do.

Likewise, offer to help other members of your household whenever you can. There might be some tasks that you excel at more than others, and taking over the ones you're not so good at can help other people focus on what they are best at doing. If everyone you live with feels supported, there will be altogether less stress in your home, making it a more productive, positive and present environment overall.

APPLY IT!
schedule a do-it day

Grab your calendar because it's time to schedule a do-it day. "What's a do-it day?", you ask. It's a day (or at least a few hours of a day) devoted entirely to taking care of tasks on your at-home to-do list.

One do-it day a month – say the last Saturday or the fifth day of every month – is all you need to get a whole heap of tasks done in a burst of positive and present energy. Try to be consistent each month about your do-it day, make sure everyone in the house is aware of it and respects it, enlist help when you can, and turn off the TV, phone and tablet before you begin work. Stay focused and relish the sense of achievement as one by one you check things off your list.

Want to make sure you never forget to keep a do-it day? Visit danidipirro.com/books/guide for a set of free, downloadable stickers to post on your calendar, planner or diary.

FINDING TRANQUILLITY *at home*

e haven't yet touched on one of the most important aspects of making your home a positively present place. This section is about how you – yes, you! – can create tranquillity in your home even if you're surrounded by stressed housemates or children who won't sit still. As I've mentioned, when you have a calm home environment (or at least a place where you can feel relaxed at home), it's much easier to stay positive and present. But how exactly are you supposed to relax – even though you've created the right space and checked off your to-do list – when there's no switch that turns off the stress in your head or the activity around you? Fear not. Here are my suggestions for turning your mind at home, as well as your home itself, into a haven of tranquillity.

1. IDENTIFY YOUR STRESSORS

What stresses you out at home? It might be squabbling kids, work emails pinging away on your smartphone or the pressure of preparing something nutritious for dinner every night. Make a list of stressors, then think of ways to minimize them. Kids squabble? Set them each an individual task to keep them from creating conflict. Emails driving you crazy? Turn off your phone! No time to think creatively for dinner? Make a batch of something delicious on Sunday and freeze it for the weekdays. You'll never be able to completely eradicate at-home stress, but taking positive and present action to keep stress at a minimum will help you feel more in control – and calmer – at home.

2. STEP OUT

If your home seems like a whirlwind of activity and you need some peace, take yourself outside the tornado. Simply stepping into another room, out into the garden or onto a balcony or going for a quick walk around the block will give you the space to take a deep breath and focus your attention on the positive details of the present moment. Instead of ruminating about what was stressing you out, look around you. Notice nature, your breathing, or anything else positive that catches your eye. Direct your mind away from your stress and to your senses. What can you see, smell and touch? When you feel yourself more at one with the present, take another deep breath and go back to what you were doing. The act of connecting with a neutral moment may be all you need to start again with a renewed sense of peace.

reminder!
POSITIVELY PRESENT PRINCIPLE #3

Removing negativity whenever possible is an important Positively Present Principle, but there are some situations in which that's hard. If you can't remove the negativity itself, try removing yourself from the negative situation instead.

3. SCHEDULE TIME FOR MEDITATION

Although meditation might conjure up images in your mind of yogis humming to themselves in twisted poses, it doesn't have to be that way. Think of meditation as a means to find tranquillity when it seems like there is little peace around you. It's simply about sitting quietly (without distraction) and allowing the chatter in your mind to quiten down. A meditation doesn't have to be any more spiritual than that. If you have trouble calming your mind, try thinking of a word that makes you feel peaceful and hold it in your mind's eye, focusing on nothing other than the letters you visualize. Or, try finding a single point on a wall in front of you and rest your gaze on it, letting all other thoughts float away on a cloud. Or, try focusing all of your attention on your breath — slowly breathing in through your nose and out through your mouth. Whichever of these techniques feels comfortable for you, have a go at practising for as long as you are able — even if it's for only five minutes at a time.

4. INHALE CALMING SCENTS

Even if it seems like you don't have a minute to sit down for most of the day, you can imbue your home with a sense of tranquillity by using calming scents. Chamomile, passionflower, valerian root, ginseng and lavender are just some of the scents known to have calming properties. Lavender, in particular, is said to alleviate anxiety and encourage calm. Try hanging a bunch of lavender by the door to induce calm as soon as you enter your home, or light a lavender-scented candle when you finally get the kids to bed and sit down alone for the evening.

APPLY IT!
create a relaxing ritual

Having a relaxing ritual you can practise every day is an excellent way to ward off stress while at home. Here's how to create your ideal relaxing ritual:

1 Choose a time for your ritual that will work more or less every day. Perhaps your best time is as soon as you walk through the door post-work, or perhaps a bedtime wind-down ritual would work better for you.

2 Choose an activity that won't take too much time or energy to complete. For example, walk through the door, take off your shoes, slip into some sweats and read a good book for 15 minutes. Or, before you get ready for bed, slather yourself in lavender lotion, brew a cup of chamomile tea and listen to some soothing tunes.

3 Whatever ritual you choose, stick with it for at least a week. At first it might seem hard to prioritize it over dealing with the business of home, but once you've done it for a few days, you'll really start to enjoy the consistency of a little bit of dedicated bliss in your day.

4 If the ritual starts to feel stale or more of an obligation than a source of tranquillity, it's time to tweak it or try something new.

listen TO WHAT calms YOUR soul

APPLY IT!
try these tips for falling asleep

Having trouble getting to sleep? Try this trick that's worked for me for years: focus your attention on what you can hear, feel and smell while you're trying to fall asleep. Focusing on these senses distracts your mind from the rumination that can keep you awake.

Alternatively, if you need to focus on something physical to stop your mind whirring, start at your toes and tense each muscle group in turn, holding the tension briefly and then fully letting go. Work up through your body, tensing and releasing each area, until you reach your head. Then, tense all your muscles at once and release them at once. Enjoy feeling enveloped in a sense of total physical relaxation – the perfect forerunner to a sound sleep.

5. GET (OR BORROW) A PET

It's been proven that stroking a pet can reduce stress and even lower blood pressure; in some cases caring for a pet may even help overcome the effects of depression. Pets not only show unconditional love (the cat curled up on your knee; the dog so pleased to see you as you walk through the door), but they also remind you to stay in the moment because they are always focused on the present. They are also just plain cute, which will put a smile on your face even if you've had a tough day. Obviously, pets aren't for everyone (after all, owning one comes with responsibility and time commitment), but you don't have to have a pet of your own to reap the benefits animals have to offer. You can volunteer to pet-sit for a friend or family member, or visit a local animal shelter to see if staff there need a helping hand to walk or play with the animals in their care.

6. MAKE SLEEP A TOP PRIORITY

Sleeping is absolutely, without a doubt, the most important thing you can do to reduce your stress levels. When you don't get enough sleep, you get cranky, you don't think clearly, and you tend to eat things that don't fill you with good, positive energy (or am I the only one who binges on junk food when I'm tired?). The less sleep you get, the more likely you are to make mistakes, get into arguments and just generally feel out of sorts. Most of us have a certain amount of sleep that works best for us. Too much sleep can make us feel irritable, while too little can make us feel groggy and disconnected. There are heaps of apps and gadgets out there to monitor your sleep patterns and even help you to work out your ideal amount of sleep. Routine is important. Try to go to bed at the same time every night and wake up at roughly the same time every morning. Do your best to stick to your optimum sleep/wake schedule, even when temptation beckons. It's tough when you only have a few hours at the end of the day at home to do the things or see the people you love, but getting the right amount of sleep should be a top tranquillity priority.

sleep IS AN ACT OF self-love

LIVING WITH *crankiness*

N o matter how angelic your children, spouse or housemates usually are, you're bound to encounter a few moments (or days) filled with crankiness. We all have good days and bad days. You might have an amazing day of bright, sunny skies, only to be greeted at your door by someone whose day was filled with grumbling grey clouds. How in the world are you supposed to stay positive when the people around you are spewing negativity? How are you supposed to enjoy your moments at home when others there seem miserable? Crankiness, in ourselves as well as in others, stands in the way of creating a positive and present home, but it's a part of life. Even the most positive people have down days – and that's OK. Remember: living a positively present life isn't about being happy every single minute of every single day. It's about managing every situation in a positive and present way. Here are five tips for making the best of your time at home, even when those around you aren't feeling quite so positive.

1. SPEAK WITH LOVE

It's tough not to speak in a voice that reflects the tone of someone who is being negative, sharp or unkind. It's almost an instinct to respond in the same way we've been spoken to – but this can only make situations worse. Remind yourself that you have stumbled into a bad time for the other person (perhaps a single moment, perhaps a day or sometimes something more protracted), and pause before you respond. Breathe, count to ten and remind yourself that a positive mindset is a choice you can make, a choice that will benefit you in this moment. With a positive frame of mind, respond with kind words spoken in a loving tone – or at least a level one. The less negativity you put into the conversation, the easier it will be to transform it from negative to positive. If it's really hard to speak kindly (as it can be sometimes when someone is really cranky), try to keep your distance. Saying nothing is better than saying something unkind or inflammatory.

THERE IS *beauty* IN SILENCE

2. REVERSE YOUR REACTION

Instead of reacting instantly to a cranky person's words or actions, consider for just a moment what your knee-jerk response might be and imagine yourself making the exact opposite reaction. For example, if you were about to yell, visualize yourself speaking in a soft, calm voice or giving them a hug. Sometimes responding in the exact opposite way to the way you want to react (even when it's difficult to do so) can lead to a much more positive interaction, and it will also help you keep your inner state calm and collected.

reminder!
POSITIVELY PRESENT PRINCIPLE #4

Love and appreciate who you are by trying not to worry so much about what others are thinking or why they are acting negatively. Just give yourself a chance to stay positive.

(Note: This point does not apply when you want to speak positively. Never reverse a positive reaction!)

3. DON'T TAKE IT PERSONALLY

It takes enormous strength of character not to take someone else's negative words personally, imagining that a snappy tone or unkind word is entirely about you. But take a step back. Consider how you feel when you've had a bad day. You might be a little less kind and a little snippier with those you live with. It's not about them; it's just that you're tired, frustrated or upset (or a combination of all three). Keeping in mind that we often lash out at those we love best may help you not take another's negativity to heart.

4. FOCUS ON YOURSELF

More often than not, when we're cranky, the last thing we want is someone asking, "Are you OK? Is everything alright? Why are you in a bad mood?" Instead of peppering someone with questions, take the crankiness as a sign to step back and spend some one-on-one time with yourself. Pick up a book and go into another room to read, take a nice long bath to relax yourself, or call up a friend you haven't talked to in a while. In doing this you'll avoid getting sucked into someone else's negative state of mind, and you'll give that person the space they need to sort out whatever they're going through.

5. CREATE A CODE WORD

Has someone ever taken you by surprise by asking, "Are you in a bad mood?" Sometimes crankiness creeps up on us and we don't even notice it. Talk to your housemates about creating a code word you can each use to mean "Hey there! You're being a little cranky right now and I'm not sure if you realize it. I'm going to keep my distance, but find me if you need me." (You could create another that warns people when you know you're feeling cranky, too.) Code words help to raise everyone's empathy levels so you avoid combative situations. They have another powerful benefit, too: when you find yourself using them a lot, you know there are a lot of negative moments in your (or someone else's) life. Perhaps it's time to take a closer look at what's causing bouts of crankiness – and make changes if necessary.

APPLY IT!
make a bad-mood buster box

Cohabiting with a cranky person can make it really tricky to stay positive, but a great way to cope with occasional crankiness is to remind yourself of the reasons why you enjoy spending time with this person. To do this, create a bad-mood buster box.

1 Find a small box or jar and cut up scraps of paper to place beside the box. Every time the cranky person does something you like, something that makes you happy or something to make you laugh, write it down on a piece of paper and put it in the box.

2 When you find yourself faced with that person's cranky mood, look through the box to remind yourself of all the reasons why that person is awesome. You'll start to feel grateful for all the positive moments you've shared – and you'll be reminded that this mood is just a passing thing.

3 Visit danidipirro.com/books/guide for a free bad-mood buster download sheet. You could even empty the box from time to time and stick all the notes in a scrapbook of reflections on why the person you live with is so great.

HAVING A
home-based HOBBY

Throughout my life I've had one hobby or another – from making collages and music mixes to reading, illustrating, designing and Instagramming. Having a hobby (even when you feel you already have plenty to do) has tons of positive benefits (see opposite for seven of them). What better way to relax than to do the things you love doing – things you might not have an opportunity to do on a daily basis at work or college? And what better place to do those things than at home? Although a hobby doesn't have to be home-based to have positive benefits, a hobby at home is available to you whenever you have spare time and can dip into it, making it more likely you'll actually engage in it often. Every hobby I've ever had has helped me stay more in touch with the moment by allowing me to do what makes me feel positive and inspired. And when I engage in a hobby at home, I create a stronger connection not only with myself and what I enjoy doing, but also with the place in which I live.

If you don't already have a hobby, the thought of adding something else into your schedule may seem overwhelming. However, here are some ideas for starting a hobby at home that make it easier to reap the rewards rather than feeling you have simply added more to your to-do list.

1. FIND SOMETHING YOU LOVE TO DO

Spend some time thinking about what you love to do at home. Reading, writing, drawing, model building, doing puzzles, cooking, knitting, sewing, scrapbooking, dancing, singing and so on are all good examples. Search online for more ideas, and ask your friends. Don't worry if nothing grabs your interest right away. Try to keep an open mind and sample some hobbies to see how you respond to them once you actually start practising them. When you find something you love, stick with it. The more you love what you're doing, the more likely you are to value and enjoy the time you make for it.

seven benefits
OF A HOBBY

Having a hobby is good for your mind and your body because it ...

1 ... encourages you to take a break with a purpose. Practising a hobby gives you time out from your humdrum daily life, but it's action-oriented so you feel you're accomplishing something even while you're relaxing.

2 ... offers an outlet for your stress. It can fully absorb your attention, focusing your mind on something positive that's unrelated to the stressful things in your life.

3 ... provides a positive challenge. It encourages you to explore new ideas and activities that may stimulate you, without the pressure of a work or college project.

4 ... unites you with others. Even if you engage in a solo activity, you're bound to find others who share your passion or admire your efforts.

5 ... has physical health benefits. Engaging in enjoyable activities during downtime has been associated with higher levels of positivity and lower levels of depression and blood pressure.

6 ... keeps you in the present. When you're doing something you really enjoy, the hours can magically fly by. Instead of worrying about the future or dwelling on the past, you'll find yourself completely engrossed in the now.

7 ... promotes "eustress". That's the positive kind of stress that makes you feel excited about what you're doing and about life.

2. ENCOURAGE A GROUP ACTIVITY

I'm one of those introverted types who prefers a hobby I can do alone, but if you feel that a hobby might use up valuable time for spending with the people you live with, consider an activity you can enjoy together. Baking and board games are perfect for a family, while a household book club will allow individual time reading as well as group time discussing. Group activities provide all of the benefits of having a hobby with the added advantage of social interactions that can strengthen bonds with your loved ones or housemates.

reminder!
POSITIVELY PRESENT PRINCIPLE #6

Focus on what inspires you by taking conscious note of the activities that make you feel particularly enlivened. When you find something that holds your interest, make doing that activity a priority.

3. TURN OFF ELECTRONIC DEVICES

Distraction is the enemy of being fully present, so turn off your phone, email, TV and any other potential electronic distraction while engaged in your chosen activity. If you need to use a device for the hobby (for example, if your hobby is writing poetry and you do this on your computer), try turning off the WiFi while you write so you can properly get into the flow and avoid derailing your concentration.

4. SCHEDULE IT

With all you have to get done in a given week or month, finding time to fit in something that's not essential can be tough. That's why it's a good idea to schedule your hobby. When you put it on the calendar (even just half an hour a week, or an hour a month), just as you would a meeting or an appointment, you give it value and remind yourself that your hobby is just as worthwhile as any of your other tasks – in fact, it's even more worthwhile than many of them because it truly helps you stay positive in the present. However, don't focus so much on scheduling things that you eliminate all spontaneity from your life. When you can, grab five minutes to do something you love doing, whether that's singing in the shower or dancing around your bedroom or just watching the clouds go by ...

5. START SOMETHING NEW

If you're like me, you'll grow to love your hobby, but that doesn't mean you should let it get stale or become habitual. Every few months or so, start a new project based on the hobby you already know and love. For example, if you love building model airplanes, perhaps you want to try your hand at building a doll house instead. If you adore reading biographies, maybe you want to give historical fiction a shot. Or, if you love sketching and drawing, maybe it's time to see how you like painting. By starting a new kind of project, you'll maintain your interest levels and focus, as well as expand your talents and challenge your mind to think in new and exciting ways.

APPLY IT!
hunt down your hobby

If you already have an at-home hobby that you love, that's amazing! But if you don't have a hobby, want to pick up a new one, or want to revitalize a pastime that's gone stale, this activity is for you.

1 What was your favourite activity or pastime when you were a child? What did you like about it? Would you like to give it another try?
2 If you could have a whole day without interruptions, what would you spend it doing?
3 What would your dream job consist of? Is there any way to turn aspects of that job into a hobby?
4 What are some activities you've seen others enjoying and have always wanted to try yourself?

Visit danidipirro.com/books/guide for a printable version of these questions and for a list of possible hobbies that might interest you.

WHAT MAKES YOU FEEL
YOU FEEL
alive?

CHAPTER TWO

being positively present at work

T here's a reason why the word "work" is not only a noun but also a verb meaning "to exert effort". Work – whether you love it, hate it or don't really think much about it – requires exertion. Every day you've got to get up, get yourself together and get moving toward your job. And the thing about a job is it's not a one-time deal (at least, not for most people). For most of us, a job is an every day, five-days-a-week, at least eight hours a day kind-of-thing. If you dislike your job, making the most of your moments at work becomes very challenging. I've been there. I've had quite a few jobs I absolutely despised. Even though I often found the silver lining in some stellar co-workers, I couldn't get over the fact that I was miserable every single day. Some nights I would literally cry myself to sleep because I was so distressed at the thought of waking the next morning to go to work (not very present-minded of me, I know!). In this chapter I'm going to show you how being more positive and more present can help you make the most of any work situation, cope with the inevitable challenging personalities and stressful times you'll encounter, and show off your skills to create a career that motivates you to get up in the morning.

If you have a job you love (I have one of those now, too), you probably already know what it's taken me a while to learn: just because your job is awesome doesn't mean *working* is awesome. Yes, there are moments of pure bliss (when I look around my little at-home office, I often think, "I'm so lucky to be doing what I love. This is amazing!"). But there are many times when doing what I love is hard work. No matter what you do for a living, it's hard to stay positive and present while doing it *all the time*.

You might think, "If only I had a different job ..." or "If only I didn't have to deal with my boss ..." or "If only that one annoying co-worker would quit ...", but do you really want to sit around waiting for something to change? You might have to wait for some things to change (getting a new job or a promotion, for example, doesn't happen overnight), but one thing you can change immediately is your own attitude.

I won't lie and say it's always easy to stay in the moment as you do your job, but the more you can master the art of staying positive and present in the workplace, the more productive, motivated and inspired you'll become. And you can use that productivity and motivation to improve your current career or even make a move to a new one.

MAKING THE MOST OF *what you do*

S o you've got a job! Hooray! It might not be your dream job – or even what you'd necessarily hoped for in a career path – but it's a job and that's something to be proud of. Nonetheless, while you're working you might find it a bit difficult to stay in the moment and embrace a positive attitude. After all, you're spending your time working instead of "playing", possibly taking orders from someone or maybe giving orders to others (not as much fun as it sounds), and probably surrounded by some cranky people as well as some happy ones. Many aspects go into influencing your day-to-day work experience – from the commute to the to-do list to whatever is going on in your personal life. With so much coming together to influence a single workday, no wonder it's hard to make the most of the moments at the office (or whatever space you do your work in)!

what is work?

Throughout this chapter, I often refer to work in the standard nine-to-five job sense. You know, the kind with an office, a boss and a bunch of co-workers. But if that's not your work experience, don't think the advice won't be relevant to you. You can apply most of the strategies to any work situation – and even to life in general. So, whatever job you do – mother, accountant, electrician, beekeeper – keep reading!

Whether you love what you're doing or long for a change, the best way to make the most of your career is to start making the most of your current situation. The more you strive to appreciate your day-to-day work experience, the more you'll enjoy the moments you spend at your workplace. It's a virtuous circle! And the more you enjoy the moments you spend at work, the easier it becomes to stay positive and present on a daily basis. And remember: like attracts like; or, in this case, positive people attract positive people. If you dedicate yourself to making your daily work experience a positive one and strive to stay in the moment, you'll draw others with similar mindsets to you or maybe even start to have a positive effect on others' mindsets. Engaging with like-minded co-workers is a great way to get through the day. Here are my top tips.

reminder!
POSITIVELY PRESENT PRINCIPLE #5

Adopt an attitude of gratitude at work by seeing your job as an opportunity to learn something new each and every day. New insights are lurking everywhere in your workplace – embrace them and be thankful for them.

1. LEARN FROM WHAT YOU DO

Even if you don't love your job, you can learn from it. Any job, loved or hated, teaches "stickability" (seeing things through to the end), co-operation and how to overcome challenges. Being around others – probably not of your choosing – teaches important people skills, from how to collaborate, negotiate and compromise with those who view things differently to how to get a job done with someone who would rather chat away the day. Processing so many viewpoints and opinions from our co-workers opens our eyes to new ways of thinking. Every day, walk into your office and open your mind, eyes and ears to all the positive things you can learn from your job and working environment while you're there.

2. TAKE A BREAK

Relaxing at work might seem like an oxymoron, but it's good for your productivity to take regular breaks during the working day. Giving your mind and body a chance to stop, even for a few minutes, can refresh your powers of reasoning and help you see things from new perspectives. It can even encourage innovation. If you have a sedentary job, get up and stretch your legs every hour or so. Try little breaks with rewards to motivate you to stay positive. For example, take a few minutes to read a handful of pages of a book or spend a minute or two looking at an inspiring website. And try not to be tempted to eat your lunch at your desk, no matter how busy you are. In the middle of the day, get out of your usual working space, give yourself a proper change of scenery and refuel with something delicious and nutritious.

3. IMPROVE YOUR COMMUTE

In an ideal world we'd all work in easy strolling distance from where we live, so traffic jams, packed commuter trains and heaving buses would have no impact on how we begin the day. However, in the real world most of us have some distance to travel – at least some of the time (even home workers may have to go to meetings) and an unpleasant commute can wreak havoc on even the most positive mind. You can aim to make your commute as enjoyable as possible by doing one (or more!) of the following:

- Leave earlier or later to avoid peak traffic hours.
- Take a more scenic route.
- Keep switching your routes so you don't get bored.
- Carpool with a co-worker (chatting makes time go faster!).
- Listen to a captivating audio book.
- Use scent to relax. Find a car freshener with a calming fragrance or keep a sachet of dried lavender leaves in your bag.
- Stock-pile relaxing, inspiring tunes to use as your travelling music.
- Give yourself a little treat on your way to and from work – maybe a cup of tea on the way in and a nibble of chocolate on the way home.

4. SAY WHAT YOU NEED TO SAY

When you say what needs to be said at the office – providing constructive criticism to others (politely, of course), suggesting your own ideas in meetings, or challenging something you know isn't right instead of staying quiet – you validate the time you spend doing your job and you boost your self-respect. Speaking up is a way to exercise your autonomy over your role in the workplace, and it empowers you to feel some control over your whole career. You may also inspire others to speak up – opening opportunities for healthy, frank discussions and making others feel more positively present.

listen
TO YOUR
HEART, THEN

speak
UP FOR
YOURSELF

5. OFFER YOUR HELP

Helping others struggling with their own workload, even if you have only 30 minutes spare, is not just a friendly thing to do, it's also a great way to build positive relationships with your colleagues. And positive relationships will help foster a happier, more productive work environment. Making an offer to help someone outside of your usual work circle – perhaps to someone new in the office or someone with whom you often find it difficult to connect – is a particularly positive way to build bridges that might help both of you in the future. And after all, who knows when your paths might cross in the years ahead?

6. ASK FOR HELP

Asking for help is not a sign of weakness nor is it an indication that you're unable to do your job. On the contrary, it shows strength and self-awareness, and is another way to form positive bonds with your co-workers. It opens communication channels and shows others you're not too proud to admit you can't do everything on your own. Asking for help – and getting it – will help cut down on your stress levels, making you feel more positive about your job and your workplace. And lower stress coupled with positive experiences can help you become more productive overall.

7. SEVER OLD HABITS

If you've been at a job for a while, you probably know just how easy it is to slip into habitual routines and patterns. Think about the behavioural habits you have in the office. Perhaps you always arrive early to meetings only to find others' lateness irritating; or perhaps you always begin the day feeling frazzled because you're not sure which project to take on first. Make a list of your work behaviour patterns. Which of them have negative effects on your ability to be positive? Now think of ways to transform these negative habits into positive ones. For example, use the time you have before others arrive at a meeting to read back through your notes; or, at the end of each day, create a list of tomorrow's to-do items in order of urgency so you know how to begin the next day. You may have positive habits that don't cause you any stress – but try mixing these up, too. Drink tea instead of your usual coffee; let someone else lead the meeting if you're usually the one in charge; don't walk straight past your boss's office in the morning – pop your head round the corner and say hello.

I know, "work" and "fun" might sound like opposites, but keep an open mind (Positively Present Principle number 1!). Use the following tips to help you bond with your colleagues and make your working environment a fun, more connected place (enlist the help of your boss or human resources department if you need to).

• Host a monthly social or party – in the office if you can, so everyone can come. Have food delivered or ask everyone to bring a favourite dish.

• Choose one employee a month at random (names in a hat) and ask that person to circulate a "Who am I?" factfile about themselves, peppered with interesting or funny facts.

• Hold meetings outside when the weather is nice, giving everyone a chance to get some Vitamin D from the sunshine and breathe in the fresh air.

• Start a monthly book club, a dining club (go out for lunch once a month) or a sport league (a bowling night with regular teams works well).

8. DON'T LIVE FOR YOUR JOB

You might spend most of your life at work, but work doesn't have to be your whole life. Outside of the office, fill your time with interests, hobbies and relationships that fulfil and motivate you. Remind yourself every day how these are the parts of your life that define you and give you the strength to stay positively present at work. Try to have something to look forward to – meeting a loved one, cooking a meal, watching a movie, doing some gardening or whatever inspires you – when you leave the office every day.

DEALING WITH CHALLENGING *personalities*

hether you work in an office building bursting with people, in a one-room office with just a few others, or even on your own, interactions with co-workers and clients can be wonderful and inspiring and motivating ... but they can also be riddled with pent-up emotions, competitiveness and strong opinions. Unfortunately, negativity is all too prevalent in many work environments because there are so many different personalities coming together to handle a variety of (often stressful) tasks. Staying positively present at work is an essential tool for making the best of stressful situations. Sometimes unpleasantness is the result of someone else's bad day. Sometimes it's the result of clashing opinions. And sometimes it might just be that you and the other person are not a match made to click. You might have trouble with someone you have to work closely with. Or, you might be irritated by someone you barely encounter, but who happens to have an aggravating habit (I'm talking to you, guy I used to work with who clipped his nails at his desk ... Gross!). Or, you might struggle with an overbearing or micromanaging boss.

Like it or not, the work you have to do may rely heavily on interaction with other people. So, you need to get comfortable with the people you're around day after day. Even if you love the people you work with (and I hope you do), you're bound to face some bad days or situations. Even our closest comrades may be snappy, lazy or irritating at times. If you try to change other people's behaviour, you're likely

reminder!
POSITIVELY PRESENT PRINCIPLE #2

Be aware of – and willing to shift your thoughts – by zeroing in on your own positive attitude. If you feel you are surrounded by negative colleagues in your workplace, remember that you always have the option to choose positive thinking, no matter the actions or attitudes of the people around you.

to get frustrated. Instead, take control of your own responses. Try to see the good in those around you and set your mind to creating an agreeable environment for yourself. You'll find that staying positive (and not wanting to run from those you work with) makes it much easier to accomplish work-related tasks and achieve career goals. Each irritating person or behaviour is an opportunity to develop patience and compassion, two traits that help to create a more positive and present existence. Here are some ideas for coping with those challenging colleagues.

1. FOCUS ON YOURSELF

Other people's behaviours, actions and reactions can deeply influence how you feel – but only if you let them. The next time you find yourself in a frustrating situation or with an irritating person, ask yourself the following questions: "How is my body reacting to the emotions of others?", "How do I want my body to react?", "What do I really think of the situation?", "How can I focus more on my own thoughts and less on the reactions

positivity
IS ALWAYS
AN OPTION

WHAT IS *your body* TELLING YOU?

of others?" You have the power to focus on yourself – and to transform your mindset into whatever you want to it to be. No matter what others are doing, you can choose to steer away from their negativity and toward your own positivity.

2. FIND YOUR MANTRA

Having a mantra – a key word or phrase you repeat to yourself when you're feeling anxious – can be useful when dealing with difficult individuals at work. Instead of absorbing the negativity, focus on a word that represents how you want to feel – positive, calm, tranquil and so on – and repeat it in your mind whenever you feel frustrated or overwhelmed by others. Your mantra encourages you to focus on what's happening within you (rather than on external factors) and gives you a way to centre yourself in the moment and continue to engage with your colleagues, however challenging their behaviour.

3. REMOVE YOURSELF MENTALLY

A bit of negativity can be bearable, but when it gets too much, or when you have little or no control over a situation, it's OK to let your mind take a break. Take your mind somewhere else and think of things that make you feel calm and happy, such as memories of a favourite holiday, how it feels to have the wind in your hair or sand at your feet. This isn't to say you should zone out every time the going gets tough, but it's fine to let your mind visit a more positive place for a moment. (Don't be afraid to call time out physically, too. If you feel overwhelmed by negativity, suggest a coffee break. When the discussion resumes, emotions may be more constructive.)

4. REALIZE THINGS CAN CHANGE

Consider some of the other relationships you've had in your life. They've probably had some ups and downs, right? Work relationships are no different. The people you struggle to get along with now might be some of your closest confidantes in the future (or at least they might become much more tolerable). A lot feeds into how people interact with one another – what's going on in their personal lives, what projects they're currently working on and so on – and when things in your life or someone else's life change, so too might the relationship. This isn't to say that all relationships will change – some are just never going to be ideal – but it doesn't hurt to consider the possibility that someday the interactions you have with various people might become more positive. Considering this may help improve current situations.

5. FIND YOUR POSITIVITY BACK-UP

Positive emotions are contagious, so find co-workers who share your enthusiasm for what you do (or make you feel enthusiastic about what you do). After you've had a negative interaction, try to find a positive work friend to boost yourself back up. If you know you have a meeting coming up with your tricky boss, make a date to follow it with coffee with one of your more optimistic colleagues. If you work alone, follow tricky interactions with suppliers/clients/buyers with an activity that re-establishes your love of what you do. Are you grateful for a recent deal? Write a letter of thanks to the other party. Do you love to get organized? Spend some time sorting your desktop. Or just do something positive that makes you feel good – indulging in a little treat of chocolate, stepping outside for some fresh air or making a quick call to a friend can put you in a more positive frame of mind.

APPLY IT!
play positive points

Whenever you find it difficult to cope with your challenging colleagues, play the positive points game. Give yourself a point for every time you find something positive about a difficult colleague. For example, your co-worker might drive you crazy with her over-the-top criticism, but she *does* always bake the best cakes when birthdays come around. For an extra thrill, give yourself a little reward (a cup of coffee or a mid-afternoon cookie) when you reach ten positive points.

good vibes
ARE CONTAGIOUS

SURVIVING A stressful week

hether it was because of a huge presentation coming up, an all-or-nothing meeting with important clients, or just a million little things to get done, you've probably experienced the hell that is "the most stressful week of the year". You know what I'm talking about! It's the week of only headaches, problems, mishaps and cranky co-workers. It's the week when you say, "This is it! I'm going to quit for real this time!" (But you probably don't, because when the week is through, you more likely realize this gig really isn't all that bad.)

let THE LITTLE THINGS go

Your worst week might be predictable, coming during a certain month or time of year (think of the tax accountant at the end of the financial year), or it might take you by surprise, pummelling you with tasks when you thought you had everything under control. However and whenever your most stressful work weeks arrive, if you want to stay positively present, you need to manage them. Start with figuring out the best ways for handling your unique stress. Do you need to let off steam with physical exercise? Or, are you someone who needs to escape into a peaceful place within yourself? If you're not sure what works best for you, here are a few techniques to get you started and help to make it easier to stay in the moment (no matter how stressful that moment might feel!).

1. LET IT SLIDE

This doesn't mean turn your back on the big things in your working life (you have to do that presentation, even if it's stressing you out). It means letting the less important things slide for a while. Don't panic about not answering that email about sales figures for something that is already in the market; or about tidying your desktop. You'll have a chance to catch up on non-essential tasks when the stressful week is over. If you're worried about forgetting these things, note them in your diary or on your to-do list.

2. TAKE BREAKS AND DEEP BREATHS

Taking breaks is essential to staying positive and making the most of your moments. You'll focus better on the tasks in hand, even the stressful ones, if you refresh your focus often. Just a walk around the block or riding the elevator to the top floor and looking at the skyline will do. When you can't make time for a break, take a few long, deep breaths to soothe yourself. Your boss throws another big task at you? Take a few long, deep breaths. Co-worker snaps at you when you offer to help out? Take a few long, deep breaths. Irritating email arrives in your in-box? Take a few long, deep breaths. Small actions can make a big difference in bringing you back to the present moment.

3. BOND WITH THOSE AROUND YOU

Are you the only one in the thick of this stressful maelstrom, or do you have co-workers who are managing the load, too? If the latter, think of this week as an opportunity to focus on creating or strengthening bonds with those you work with. Commiserate about your sky-high stress levels (even laugh about them!), or find innovative ways to make a dull task fun (a light-hearted contest could be a good idea – divide up that stack of data-inputting and see who can get to the end of their batch first). A stressful environment is so often a breeding ground for irritation and discontent, but with the right attitude, you have the power to transform negative situations into positive relationships.

4. DO SOMETHING NICE FOR SOMEONE

OK, I know you're stressed and probably thinking, "Someone should be doing something nice for *me!*" However, doing something nice for someone else – it can be as small an action as asking someone how she's doing or holding open the door for a co-worker – gives you a feel-good mood boost. Even a little lift in your mood can have a big impact on bringing down your stress levels.

reminder!
POSITIVELY PRESENT PRINCIPLE #5

Remember to adopt an attitude of gratitude, even in the midst of a stress-filled week. Steer clear of negative thoughts by being thankful for all the good things you have (even if they're non-work related). This stressful week is just a tiny part of the intricate, beautiful landscape of your life.

5. DO ONE THING AT A TIME

When you have ten tasks (or 20!) on your to-do list, you probably want to do as many of them at the same time as possible (who can't do online research at the same time as making calls to clients?). But instead of trying to keep as many balls in the air as possible, spend a short time prioritizing what you need to do. Then start at the top of your list and work your way down, ignoring all interruptions to focus on each task, one at a time. Studies show that doing one thing at a time is a more productive way to get things done (take that, multi-tasking!), and it also helps quell that panicky voice in your head that's screaming, "OMG! I have so much to get done today!!!" Juggling the balls can freak you out; throwing and catching just one is easy!

juggle

ONE BALL
AT A TIME

6. FOCUS ON THE NOW

Why would you want to focus on the now when the present situation is stressing you out? Actually, it's often not the present moment that's stressful; it's worrying about the "what ifs". What if everything doesn't look right for the presentation? What if you don't get this done in time? Focus on the tasks you have to accomplish (one at a time!) and have faith that everything will work out the way it's supposed to. Even if it doesn't, you know a negative attitude would never have helped you, so by staying positive and focusing on the now you'll be sure you did your best to help yourself.

7. APPRECIATE WHAT'S WORKING

Don't let a specifically stressful situation sour the good things in your life. Focus on what's going right at work – both inside and outside of the stressful situation. Did you do well on a presentation even though it was extremely difficult to put together? Did you nail a tough sale? Did you challenge yourself in a new way? In the midst of a hard day, did your boss offer words of encouragement? Take a moment or two and actually write a list of what's going well to help you keep things in perspective and as a reminder to stay positive and present.

APPLY IT!
bring back the best week

Spend five or ten minutes writing about the best working week you've ever had, considering the following questions:

1 What happened during that week to make it so enjoyable?
2 Who was part of that great week?
3 How did it feel when things were going really well?
4 What did you do (or not do) to make sure things stayed positive?

After writing about your experience, repeat to yourself: "This will happen again." Your current week might be super-stressful, but there is always the potential for a great week in which every day feels like a sunshine-soaked Friday.

focus ON WHAT'S working AT WORK

SHOWCASING *your talents*

ou probably spend most of your time during the week at work, which is why it's so important to make work a positive influence in your life. Some people are lucky enough to have a job that helps them explore and grow their unique talents and skills (the artist who paints all day; the lawyer who is a deft negotiator), but for many of us the connection between our unique talents and our career isn't as obvious. Why is it so important to showcase your skills and talents in the workplace? First, your skills are usually a product of what you enjoy or are good at doing, so the more they form part of your working day, the more you'll love your work and be positively present while you're doing it. Second, showcasing what you're brilliant at will bring your unique talents to the attention of your supervisors and colleagues, making them more likely to turn to you for that type of work. And, third, acknowledging your talents to yourself is an excellent way to boost your self-esteem. The better you feel about yourself, the more productive, positive and motivated you'll be both at work and elsewhere.

Showcasing your skills isn't about arrogance. It's about recognizing your strengths and loving yourself enough to share them with the world without hesitation. Knowing – and showing – what you're good at is a form of self-love, a way not only to make your work life better, but also to help others and to improve your relationship with yourself. If you've been keeping your skills and talents under wraps, it's time to let them shine and to show those you work with just what you can accomplish given the right opportunity. Here's how you can get started.

1. BELIEVE IN YOUR ABILITIES

No one knows you better than you, so it's up to you to know and believe in yourself, first and foremost. Yes, your co-workers might applaud your abilities and tell you you're a shining star, but you won't believe their praise until you yourself believe you're worthy of it. To help you recognize what you're good at, aim to be as present and self-aware as possible as you go about your work, paying close attention to what you do well.

2. TAKE CARE OF YOUR MIND AND BODY

If you feel physically unwell or if your mind is buzzing with stress, you won't be able to make the most of your talents and skills. Treat your body with respect: pay attention to how it feels and respond appropriately. Working non-stop through the day and into the night is not great for your health (or your productivity). Take breaks at work, especially for lunch, and try to get enough sleep at night. It's also a good idea to make time in your week for exercise. Getting physically fit will boost your confidence, which in turn will encourage you to show others just what you can achieve.

reminder!

POSITIVELY PRESENT PRINCIPLE #4

While you may mostly think of self-love as a state of mind, you can also love and appreciate who you are by treating your body with kindness. Show yourself love by keeping your body in good working order, eating healthy foods, exercising appropriately and resting when you need to. A healthy body also means a healthy mind – putting you in a better place to showcase your talents.

3. DO WHAT YOU DO WELL

Ask your boss if you can spend more time doing tasks that highlight your skills and talents. For example, if you're wonderful at maths, but your job is mainly filing, perhaps you can help out in accounts for a short time each week. Take every opportunity to show others what you're good at doing. If you only *talk* about how great you are, you might seem arrogant, so reveal your skills through what you do rather than what you say.

4. LEAP OVER OBSTACLES

It's often easier for your superiors to maintain the status quo rather than to acknowledge you might be better in another role. Don't let that deter you! Find ways of showing your skills. For example, if you're a great writer but you don't do much writing in your line of work, start up a department newsletter and email it out to everyone. Or, start a blog on work-related topics and send everyone the link with a request to follow you. Get creative about letting people know where your strengths lie.

5. DO WHAT FEELS RIGHT FOR YOU

Stay true to yourself by sticking to your core values (such as honesty or generosity). Showcasing your skills is key, but it's just as important to honour your values. You can do

this by highlighting your talents in a way that resonates with your soul. If your boss thanks you for a successful project, for example, there's no reason why you can't acknowledge the colleagues who helped you. It will show you're confident about the value of your own contribution, as well as letting your team know how much you appreciate them.

6. ACCEPT PRAISE GRACIOUSLY

Try not to shy away from the praise that is due to you or pass it off to someone else. Your talents earned it and you deserve to take full ownership of what you have accomplished, reinforcing your abilities in the minds of others. Accept every kind word and compliment graciously, and remind yourself that you're worthy of every one.

APPLY IT!
build a brag book

It's important to have a place where you can record your skills and talents. You don't have to share it with anyone (at least, not right away). Buy a notebook or create a document on your computer and separate it into two sections. In the first, list your general skills and talents (good at communicating, organized, always prompt and so on). In the second, list specific events or moments when you've showcased your skills (when you landed a big client, maintained a positive attitude during a stressful meeting or helped a colleague solve a problem).

The brag book will not only help boost your confidence, it can also help further your career. Your boss asks you why you deserve a pay rise? You have the answers right there! You're heading for an interview where you'll be asked how you've demonstrated your skills? Read your brag book before you leave for the appointment!

USING THE PRESENT TO
carve your career

areer is a funny word. It is often used to symbolize a nine-to-five job that enabled you to climb a corporate ladder until retirement. But today a lifelong career might consist of a variety of jobs, possibly spanning different industries. A career isn't linear – which means it's up to you to make it what you want it to be. Whatever you're doing now is a springboard for what you could do in the future.

If you can do almost anything with your career, where do you begin? How do you go from where you are now to where you want to be? To create a future career that meets (and perhaps exceeds) your expectations, it's important to focus not on where you want to be, but on where you are in your career right now. Staying present makes every moment meaningful, and the more meaning-filled moments you engage in while at your current position, the more opportunities you'll have to further your career in the future. (Even if you already have your dream job – that's awesome! – being present in that job will help you handle change within your role as it happens.) Here's what you need to do in the present to carve out your work life in the future.

reminder!
POSITIVELY PRESENT PRINCIPLE #6

Focus on what inspires you about your job to stay positively present in your work. Think back to what motivated you to take your present job in the first place. Was it the people? The money? The challenge? Use whatever first propelled you into the position to keep you continually inspired.

1. ASK YOURSELF WHY

By asking yourself, "Why do I enjoy aspects of what I do? And why do I dislike other aspects of it?", you can start to unearth the roots of what you really want from your career. If you can, ask yourself "why?" on a specific day each week, so you are continually checking how you feel about work. You'll soon reveal the activities, people and situations that make you feel good about what you do – and those that don't. Have a weekly check-in with yourself, asking yourself questions such as, "Why did I get upset at that meeting?" or "Why did I feel so good after that phone call with my client?"

2. IDENTIFY THE DETAIL OF WHAT YOU LOVE

What do you love most about your current job? Consider your answer closely to see what it is you really love. For example, you might think, "I really love working with people!" but on closer inspection, you might find what you really enjoy is spending time with a particular colleague. It's not people in general that you love, but a one-on-one connection with someone who motivates you on a daily basis. Only when you've discovered what specifics truly inspire you, can you think about what you'll need from your career in the future.

3. DO MORE OF WHAT MOTIVATES YOU

Is the work you're doing helping you live a more positive, more present life? What elements of the work you do make you feel excited about what you're putting out into the world? (This doesn't mean you're jumping for joy every time you have to go to work; it means that, on the whole, you feel fulfilled.) Find at least one useful task you really enjoy doing at work and make an effort to do it as often as possible. The more you think about what motivates you, the more you'll start to find those motivations manifested in your current career. Don't believe it? Give it a try and see what happens. What you focus on is what you end up seeing more of in your life.

4. ASSESS WHO YOU TRULY ARE

It's time to get personal. We often think of a career as something functional that can be separated from our true selves (the self we are at home). But who you are – the deep-down essence of you, including your personality, your emotional states and your unique abilities and ideas – actually plays a crucial role in how able you are to enjoy your work now. Self-awareness is essential for stepping out on the right career path. Be honest with yourself. For example, you might want to be outgoing, but are you really, or do you prefer projects that enable you to keep to yourself? You might be a people person who loves the idea of leading a team, but do you hate making decisions that might impact others? What about your job draws out the true you, for all to see and love? How can you cultivate more opportunities for that to happen in your career? Consider these questions and you'll be closer to understanding what actions to take and choices to make at work.

APPLY IT!
visualize your dream job

Create a vision board by either drawing, cutting out from magazines, or printing out images of – or words about – what you want in your career. Consider the various aspects of your career: your boss, your location, your salary, your benefits and your freedom (to name just a few!). Paste these items on a piece of paper or cardboard and put it somewhere private but where you can easily take a look at it every day. The more you know about (and focus on) what you want, the more likely you are to see it manifested in reality.

DON'T QUIT YOUR DAY DREAM

MAKING WHAT YOU LOVE *what you do*

L ife is far too short to waste time doing what you don't love, and doing what you love is one of the most powerful ways to create a positively present life. The more you love what you're doing, the more you love your life. And the more you love your life, the easier it is to stay in the moment and focus on the positive.

But first you need to know what you love to do – and you have to be very specific about this. For me, it's always been writing. I knew I wanted to be a writer, and for years I worked in jobs that involved writing – but I never loved those jobs. I was technically doing what I loved to do, but writing in general wasn't my passion. It wasn't until I started PositivelyPresent.com that I realized what I was truly passionate about – writing about and helping others achieve a more positive, more present life.

Knowing *exactly* what you love to do isn't always super-straightforward – sometimes it takes years of trial and error before you find that one thing you feel inspired to do every single day. Once you've found what you love to do, it's up to you to find a way to take it from something you love to do to something you actually do *as a job*. To do that you need a plan. Here's my advice for making the journey from "having a job" to "doing what you love".

1. DRAW YOUR MAP

Visualizing how you'll get from where you are to a more positive place in your career will both inspire you and show you the way. It can also guide you back to where you need to be if ever you feel your career is drifting off course. Your map doesn't have to be visual – you could create a list of the specific steps that take you to where you need to go – but I like to draw my career map like a geographical map. The stages might be actual locations (such as visiting your accountant's office for tax advice), but they might also be mindsets you need to achieve, habits you feel you need to break or people you want to associate with (or disassociate from) in order to move closer to doing what you love.

2. PLAN YOUR ROUTE

Most likely, there will be more than one route to get you from where you are to where you want to be. (Let's say you want to be a graphic designer: you can either go back to college and get a degree, or you could devote time to learning on your own through online classes and workshops.) Each route will have easy stretches, as well as roadblocks (see below). Determining the right route isn't just about

reminder!
POSITIVELY PRESENT PRINCIPLE #3

Remove negativity whenever possible at work by keeping an eye out for the mental roadblocks that could cause negative thinking and impact your career. Instead of allowing yourself to be negative about what you do for a living, keep your mind open to exploring inventive ways of turning a day dream into a day job.

plotting a path; it's also about knowing the best route to take for *you*. Keep in mind that the best route might not be the fastest or most direct one. (For example, going as fast as possible might mean missing out on a valuable opportunity to learn or to connect with someone.) At every crossroads on your journey, ask "Which is the best route for *me*?"

3. LOOK FOR ROADBLOCKS

Once you have your map (or list) in hand, it's time to scan the landscape ahead for roadblocks – all the challenges you could encounter along the way. Identifying potential challenges will help you either prepare for them or, if possible, avoid them. However, don't dwell too long on what could go wrong or you might become so hung up on the potential pitfalls of travelling toward your dream job that you forget to soak up every moment of getting there.

4. GATHER YOUR SUPPLIES

Imagine preparing for a road trip. You wouldn't just hop in your car and head out on the road, would you? (OK, some of you would, and I applaud your impulsiveness, but that fly-by-the-seat-of-your-pants style doesn't work well for planning a lifelong career journey.) If you're starting a long car journey, you first need to check the engine and tyres, fill up on fuel, and stock up on snacks and water to sustain you. Similarly, before you begin your career journey, consider what essentials you'll need to take you where you want to go. Do you need a stellar support system of friends and family cheering you on? Do you need a creative outlet (such as keeping a journal) to explore new ideas and connect with inspiration? Do you need a specific amount of money in your savings account? Whatever seems essential for this journey, now's the time to gather those supplies. Above all, bear in mind that many of the supplies you need – courage, determination, a vision of your destination – are already within you.

5. STAY ON TRACK

Even if you're moving toward a future you know you'll love, it can be tough to stay on course. From keeping up your positivity, to being prepared to pass up the easy job that pays lots of money so you stay on track for the one that offers fulfilment, the

APPLY IT!
brand yourself

If you're on the road to doing what you love (or even if you're already doing what you love), this exercise is for you. Imagine yourself as you would a company's brand, which should give a clear message of what the company's about, its purpose and its ethos. Use the questions below to create your own personal brand identity. And if you don't want to write in the book, visit danidipirro.com/books/guide for a printable version of these questions.

- What do you stand for? (Your brand's message)
- How did your values or talents come to be? (The story behind your brand)
- What skills or ideas do you have to offer? (Your product)
- How will what you want to do impact others? (The audience for your brand)

challenges on the road to a job filled with inspiration, motivation and satisfaction are many, various and often unique to you. Hold your focus on the rewards of your journey, and on the positive things you'll learn and discover along the way. One way to focus on the road ahead is to create a vision board (see box, page 88) of what you hope to achieve in the future, displaying words and/or images to inspire you. Use this visual reminder of the career you hope to attain to keep you motivated. Whenever you feel yourself tempted to stray from the path, take a look at your vision board and feel re-inspired to keep going.

KEEP YOUR *eyes* ON THE ROAD *ahead*

CHAPTER THREE

being positively present in relationships

ven though our perceptions, actions and reactions are ultimately within our control, the people around us significantly influence the way we see the world, how we act and how we react. Relationships are vital aspects of our lives and they often greatly affect whether we see the world from a positive or negative perspective. There are so many different types of relationship to consider, each needing a unique set of tips and tools. We've already discussed some essential relationships – with housemates and work colleagues – and in this chapter we're going to look specifically at non-romantic, non-work-related relationships, such as those you have with friends, family members and acquaintances.

Consider a few important people in your life – for example, your best friend, your mother and your next-door neighbour – and contemplate how you behave or feel with each of those people. You're always you, of course, but different people impact you in different ways and bring out different aspects of you. You might typically feel gleeful and giggly with your best friend. You might feel child-like with your mother. Perhaps you're civil and reserved with your neighbour (or frosty, if they still haven't fixed that broken fence). The wonderful thing about relationships is that they reflect back at us the many and varied aspects of ourselves, teaching us to love and appreciate who we are in all our guises.

The key to making the most of all your relationships is knowing how to optimize them so that every interaction you have creates a positive experience in your life, even if the relationship is not ideal. In this chapter, you'll take a closer look at skills you can develop to make sure you can remain positively present in your interactions with others. You'll learn how to communicate more effectively, embrace both sociability and solitude, and use the word "no" to create positivity. You'll also think about how to stop making unhelpful comparisons with others, ride out relationship storms and know when to let go of relationships that are no longer a positive influence in your life.

Of course, some of the information, tips and techniques in this chapter could just as well apply to romantic relationships. Carry with you all the advice that's relevant to your situation, whether the relationship is romantic or platonic, but when it comes to romantic relationships, read Chapter Four, too – the wonderful, magical, complex nature of romance deserves a chapter all of its own.

COMMUNICATING *effectively*

ave you ever been in a situation in which something went wrong or was completely misunderstood owing to a lack of clear communication? Communicating with others – even when you speak the same language, were raised in similar environments or have a strong bond – is surprisingly (and often annoyingly) difficult. Because we are all such wonderfully unique beings with diverse experiences, backgrounds and opinions, no two people can really ever see things from exactly the same point of view. As much as that's an opportunity for growth and development in each of us, it's also a potential source of conflict and misunderstanding.

In your quest for a positively present life, you probably want to avoid the unnecessary drama and strife of poor communication and instead devote your time to positive, healthy relationships in which you are able to clearly and quickly understand those around you. Am I right? I thought so! Of course that's what you want, but it's not always that easy, is it? Even when it comes to those who know you well (or perhaps especially when it comes to those who know you well), effective communication rarely feels as simple as we feel it should.

Nonetheless, with a little bit of effort in applying the tips below, you'll have a much better shot at communicating clearly, effectively and in such a way that you avoid unnecessary negativity in your relationships.

1. THINK BEFORE YOU SPEAK
If someone asks you something, wait a beat before you reply or respond. A brief pause gives you a chance to really think about what you want to say or do, and it can immensely improve communication. When you pause, you give yourself a chance to

better understand what someone else has said, to formulate the thoughts you really want to convey and to find the words to convey them in a way that properly reflects your meaning.

2. BE HONEST AND OPEN

Communication is a lot less complicated if everything you say is spoken from the heart. If you are open about who you are and what you think, you will gain others' trust, which can only create clear, positive two-way communication. Of course, being honest doesn't necessarily mean saying every single thing on your mind. It means speaking truth in such a way that your relationships are enhanced by your words (that is, you don't need to tell a friend she looks awful in a particular outfit just because it's the truth, but you might want to suggest a different look).

3. DON'T RUSH COMMUNICATION

Have you ever been in a rush and put down an object (your keys, your phone, your wallet) only to then spend what feels like forever trying to find it again? When we're in a rush we misplace things – the same goes for our words. The next time you find yourself communicating with someone else (whether you're speaking, writing, texting or emailing), even if it's just a simple, everyday conversation, slow down and really pay attention to what's being said to you (don't anticipate what's being said – actually listen to or read the words carefully) and respond with care.

reminder!
POSITIVELY PRESENT PRINCIPLE #4

Love and appreciate who you are by staying true to who you are when you talk to others. You can still do this while mirroring the other person's communication style, because it's adapting *how* you communicate, not *what* you communicate, that helps you get your point across.

4. ADAPT YOUR STYLE

While your own thoughts might be perfectly, brilliantly clear to you, they might be somewhat murky to others. We all think and see the world in unique ways. If you want your ideas to be understood, you have to communicate them in a way that will be well received by those listening. Your audience might be someone close to you, but that doesn't mean they can instantly understand where you're coming from. Pay attention to how others communicate with you. Do they often use metaphors? Are they always looking for a way to showcase their ideas visually (such as using salt-and-pepper shakers at the dinner table to act out a scene from their workday)? Do they use a lot of facial expressions to convey how they're feeling? Try to mirror their communication style in order to help them better understand you. You don't need to become a clone of someone else – being positively present relies upon you being you – but working someone else's style into your own can make interactions more positive and effective.

5. PAY ATTENTION TO NON-VERBAL CUES

If you want to understand what others are really thinking or saying, you have to do more than just listen. You have to pay attention to facial expressions and body language, too. (This is why it's usually better to conduct key communication sessions in person rather than via email or text, or over the phone.) If your mother tells you she loves your new haircut, but her arms are folded and she won't meet your eye, chances are she loved your locks as they were. When your best friend tells you she's always there for you, opens her hands wide and looks you straight in the eye as she does so, you know she means every word. And also consider your own non-verbal cues. Are you a chronic arm crosser? (I am, but I'm working on it!) This defensive stance may close down communication with others. Do you find it hard to look other people in the eye? If you do, they might think you're not being entirely honest. Strive to align your actions with your words in order to increase significantly your opportunities for positive interaction with others.

6. KEEP AN OPEN MIND

Communicating clearly and succinctly is pretty tough – and neither you nor someone you're talking to will get it right all the time. If a conversation seems to be going awry, keep an open mind about the point that is trying to come across. Think of the best-case scenario rather than the worst (when your friend said that dress didn't flatter your shape, she didn't mean your body is disproportionate; she meant the dress wasn't made for you). This will help prevent miscommunication from spiralling into something negative.

Furthermore, be open-minded about how others prefer to communicate. You might like to chat, but someone else might prefer – and be more receptive to – what you have to say via email. If you have an important point to make, it's best to make it in a way that's likely to be well received.

7. FOLLOW UP YOUR COMMUNICATION

It's easy to assume whatever you've attempted to communicate has been received and understood in the exact way you intended – after all, you were perfectly clear, right? But why take that for granted? It's always a good idea to follow up by email, text or a call, to make sure that everyone is aligned – especially if messages have been re-communicated from one person to another.

Equally, if you need clarification on something, don't be afraid to ask for it. If someone is talking to you and you want to be sure you've properly understood, take a moment to repeat back to them what they've said, perhaps phrasing it in a different way just to be sure.

8. ASK FOR FEEDBACK

Feedback from those you communicate with is perhaps the best way of making sure you're constantly improving your skills. Ask friends and family to tell you how clear you've been. Talk about how you could all communicate more effectively in the future. If everyone involved in the discussion raised their communication style with just one tiny tweak, the whole interaction would become more effective.

I won't deny that hearing feedback isn't always a pleasant experience. However, the more you learn about your own communication style, the more you can work on your weak spots and highlight your strengths, making communication in relationships more positive and productive.

APPLY IT!
tune into your body's signals

Paying attention to your own body language is a great way to figure out how you're feeling when you're communicating with others. Your body language will often tell you more about how you feel than your thoughts will, helping you understand what and how you truly want to communicate. For example, if your body language tells you you're really tense, perhaps now isn't the time to begin a difficult conversation. In the following situations, learn to tune in to what your body is telling you.

1 In a heated argument, sense your heartbeat. Is it faster than normal? Feel your hands. Are they in clenched fists? Sense your muscles. Are they tense in your neck and back?

2 In a loving embrace, sense your heartbeat. Is it slow and steady? Feel your hands. Are they relaxed and open? Sense your muscles. Are they relaxed and at ease?

3 In a new situation, sense your heartbeat. Is it quicker than normal? Feel your hands. Are your palms sweaty? Sense your muscles. Do any of them feel tense?

If you notice negative physical reactions, you should pay attention to your thoughts and emotional responses. In cases where clear communication is needed, it might be best to remove yourself from a situation until you are in a calmer mental state.

LEARNING TO *let go*

o matter how much you want them to work, some relationships thrive only on negativity – and these interactions can make it difficult for you to stay positive and present. A relationship filled with more downs than ups (or downs that are much lower than its ups are high) is one you might be better off without. Unlike a romantic tie, connections with family members and friends don't usually have clear break-up points, when you know a relationship needs to be over. It's hard to "break up" with a friend or family member, but if your association continually causes more negativity than positivity, it's important to let go and give yourself an opportunity to focus your attention on more positive interactions.

Putting an end to a non-romantic connection is something we don't always have to think about. It often happens almost imperceptibly – two people simply drifting slowly apart as their lives change. This kind of end of a friendship is just part of the tapestry of life. You might look back with a twinge of sadness, but you've both moved on and you're both OK. It's when you find yourself in a continuing relationship that has you asking yourself, "Is the negativity worth the relationship I'm preserving?" that you have a choice: keep managing the situation as best you can, or let the relationship go.

There's nothing easy about coming to this realization – especially if the association is with a family member who "should" be part of your inner circle or a friend who once meant everything to you. Bear in mind that "letting go" doesn't necessarily have to mean completely removing a person from your world; sometimes what's needed is an emotional letting go, in which you become less vulnerable to the other person's negativity, no longer seek their approval and can avoid becoming caught up in any damaging dramas with them.

Here are some tips for making the end of a non-romantic relationship as easy as possible.

1. CREATE SOME SPACE

When you know a relationship needs to come to an end, a good first step to take is giving yourself some space. This doesn't mean you need to make some grand statement to announce you're backing off (that's likely to cause more drama). Start slowly – don't initiate any new plans, and politely decline invitations you are offered. If you run into one another, that's fine – be friendly, but start to build in some distance. In the meantime you'll open yourself up to cultivating other, more positive interactions.

APPLY IT!
knowing when to stay and when to go

If you're not sure about whether or not a relationship brings more positivity or more negativity into your life, answer the questions below – honestly. If you'd prefer to fill these out without marking up the book (or you want to share them with someone who might need to take a closer look at one of their relationships), visit danidipirro.com/books/guide for a printable version. These questions require a simple yes or no answer, but it's helpful also to spend time thinking of examples to illustrate your answers in order to gain even more insight. Consider the other person in your relationship and ask yourself:

- Do they act in a way that embarrasses or hurts you?
- Do they put you in uncomfortable situations?
- Do they leave you feeling emotionally drained?
- Do they bring out the worst qualities in you?
- Do they make you feel devalued as a person?
- Do they evoke negative emotions (anger, hate, envy)?
- Do they encourage you to take part in harmful activities?
- Do they treat you with disrespect and unkindness?
- Do they put little or no effort into the relationship?
- Do they seem to be in constant competition with you?
- Do they make you feel smothered and confined in any way?

2. BE HONEST BUT REALISTIC

If it's at all possible, be honest with the other person about why you can no longer spend as much time together. Consider how you'll respond if the other person asks if they've done something wrong – is honesty the best policy or is it better to leave specifics unsaid? Remember that the aim is not to punish the other person, but to improve your own positive and present life. Before you take the plunge and have that conversation, do consider how the other person might react. If you think they might act violently, or if you think the negative repercussions might impact others, go back to just keeping your distance.

3. CELEBRATE POSITIVE RELATIONSHIPS

Being around positive people is likely to keep you focused on the good aspects of your life, making it easier to hold your resolve to let go of negative ones. Distracting yourself with positive people and positive activities may also help to heal any pain of an ended relationship (the pain is OK as long as it doesn't begin to take over your life). Although these aren't romantic relationships, don't underestimate how hard it can be to let go emotionally of a friend or family member. Having a strong, positive support system can help you cope with the loss.

reminder!
POSITIVELY PRESENT PRINCIPLE #6

Focus on what inspires you, on what you love to do and what brings you joy, in order to combat the negativity of others. You can't always avoid negative interactions, but you can often escape into the activities or ideas that make you feel great.

4. REFOCUS ON YOU

You've decided a relationship needs to end because you've recognized the importance of having positive, uplifting people in your life. In doing so you've shown yourself love. Continue to appreciate yourself by focusing on the things you enjoy doing (such as hobbies, see pages 54–9). Remind yourself how much more time and energy you'll have for your favourite interests and activities now you have fewer negative influences in your life. Absorbing yourself in a pastime is a wonderful way to be totally present to the moment.

SURROUND
YOURSELF
WITH
PILLARS OF
support

EMBRACING SOLITUDE AND *sociability*

Most people fall somewhere between introvert and extrovert – perhaps with a tendency toward one or the other. But whether you consider yourself to be an introvert or an extrovert, or somewhere in-between, you can gain a great deal of insight from exploring both how it feels to be alone (solitary) and how it feels to be among other people (sociable). Having a strong relationship with yourself is the perfect foundation for building strong relationships with others. (The section on self-love on pages 132–5 has more on this.) In addition, when you feel solidarity with those around you, experiencing and learning from situations you face or enjoy together, you develop qualities that strengthen your relationship with yourself. In other words there are benefits to being both solitary and sociable – and a truly positive and present life enjoys a balance of the two.

If you consider yourself to be either an introvert or an extrovert, you might not feel like dabbling at the other end of the scale. For example, I love spending time alone and have to remind myself consciously how much I actually benefit when I'm around other people. To help those of you who lean much more to being social or to being solitary, I've rounded up five benefits of being with others and five benefits of enjoying time alone. Take a close look at the scenario that appeals least to you. Social butterflies, it's time to have some me-time; homebirds, spread your wings and venture out of the nest!

Being sociable can positively impact you because you can:

1. LEARN FROM OTHERS

The more time you spend with other people, the more you learn. They can teach you about the world (think of all the cultures, belief systems and traditions you come into contact with through others), about yourself (what you love in someone else and what makes you laugh or cry) and about how each of us is exceptional with unique qualities and foibles (an important lesson for helping you build loving, forgiving relationships).

2. LAUGH MORE OFTEN

While you don't necessarily need other people around you to be able to laugh, being sociable does seem to increase the opportunity for laughter. Besides, sharing a comic moment or two (whether while watching a movie, engaging in silly behaviour or just talking) intensifies our experience of humour. Have you ever laughed

reminder!
POSITIVELY PRESENT PRINCIPLE #2

Be aware of – and willing to shift – your thoughts by identifying whether it's the social or the solitary state that comes most naturally to you and then considering the tangible benefits that the opposite condition (being solitary or social) might hold for you.

so hard with a friend that the sound of laughter alone kept making you laugh? That's one of the best benefits of spending time with others. Sharing laughter binds us together in common joy. It is the ultimate positively present expression of a relationship.

3. EXPERIENCE NEW SITUATIONS

Let's say you have a friend who keeps horses and invites you to visit him at his stables. You might have a fondness for animals yourself, but you probably wouldn't have taken time to stop by a stable if you didn't have someone in your life interested in riding. The more time you spend with others, the more you open up your world to new experiences you might not have explored on your own. You're also more likely to try something completely new to both of you if you have a partner in adventure!

4. DEVELOP RELATIONSHIP SKILLS

The more time you spend with others, the more you strengthen your relationship skills. For example, you'll get better at empathy, learning, sharing and communicating. If social situations make you feel uncomfortable, it may be helpful to keep in mind that stepping outside your comfort zone offers you a chance to develop social skills. The more you practice, the easier such situations will become.

5. BUILD A SUPPORT NETWORK

While it's useful to make a habit of supporting yourself, there's no real substitute for the encouragement and support that come from other people. Positive support from others is a great source of energy. The more others support and believe in you, the more you'll be able to sustain the positive emotions you experience as a result of that support when you're alone. With others cheering you on, you'll feel as if you can achieve almost anything!

APPLY IT!
go solo or be sociable

Are you a social butterfly or a homebird? Whatever you consider yourself to be, choose the opposite exercise below and give it a try. See where a new way of thinking can take you!

go solo

Choose a place where you can go for a walk and be completely alone (a garden or local park might work well). Pay close attention to what you see, hear and feel. Listen closely to your own thoughts as you walk. You may uncover new ideas or experience emotions that take you by surprise. Acknowledge each one, then let it go, remembering to keep your focus fully in the present.

be sociable

Choose a few people you enjoy spending time with (or would like to get to know better) and invite them over for a meal. Find a game that appeals to you (a board game, a card game or sporting activity) and encourage everyone to take part. Interacting in this way can help you to bond with others without the focus being only on conversation (and it'll probably be fun, too!).

OTHER PEOPLE HELP YOU

learn & laugh & love

Being solitary is good for you because you can:

1. HAVE TIME TO THINK

Time spent alone provides an excellent opportunity to connect with your thoughts. When you're alone you're able to think, reflect and engage in activities (such as reading, writing or creating) likely to promote more mindfulness. And it's often when you are alone with your thoughts that inspiration will strike because, in those quiet moments, your mind is louder and you're able to listen more closely to what your heart desires.

2. DO WHAT SUITS YOUR MOOD

Alone time is a wonderful opportunity – perhaps even the *best* opportunity – to do whatever strikes your fancy or most appeals to you without having to consider the needs of others. You can listen to the music you like, watch the shows you prefer and cook up a meal that suits your tastes. When you're alone, whatever you want to do (within reason!) can be done. Bliss!

3. FULLY EXPRESS YOUR EMOTIONS

Time spent alone is just what you need to get in touch with whatever you're feeling and express those emotions fully, uninhibited by the reactions or concerns of anyone else. If you need a good, long cry, for example, you can go right ahead and have one. Being able to express your emotions fully allows you to focus intently on the present, getting in touch with how you're feeling at that moment.

4. FOCUS COMPLETELY

Although it's important to be able to focus when you're around other people (like when you're at the office), full immersion in a task is often easiest when you're on your own without distractions. Being alone and tuning in to one specific task (no multi-tasking!) often allows you to get properly into the flow of what you're doing. When you're fully engaged in that way, you're likely to be most productive.

5. BOOST YOUR CREATIVITY

Being away from people (and their many distractions) offers you a chance to explore new ways of seeing the world or a project you're working on. Some of the best out-of-the-box ideas come when you have quiet space that enables your mind to wander freely and uninterrupted. Alone time is a chance to allow your mind to search for new ideas, create innovations or find inspiration.

ENJOY YOUR TIME SPENT *alone*

SURVIVING RELATIONSHIP *storms*

Pick three of your significant relationships – perhaps with a best friend, a sibling and someone you've known since childhood – and, in your mind, map these relationships over the course of their lifetime. Perhaps you are incredibly lucky and none has ever gone through a rough patch. However, my guess is that at least one has had a period when things didn't run as smoothly as you would have liked, when you questioned whether or not the relationship was working. Not to the extent that you decided to let it go (see pages 104–7 for more on that), but just in a way that made you wonder whether it would weather the storm. Often, a bumpy time coincides with a challenging period in your or the other person's life – stressful experiences, heartache, big life changes and so on – but sometimes it's just because you've lost your shared perspective for a while and need to find your way back to one another.

Happily, the route back is really very straightforward – it's called acceptance. OK, perhaps it's not all *that* straightforward, especially when you're struggling to get along with someone, but the effort it takes to salvage a worthwhile, positive relationship is worth it. When you accept others as they are – even the parts of them you don't care for right now – you gain a sense of peacefulness that can envelop and protect the relationship while you ride out the storm. You have control over how you feel, and if you strive to see this period of time as just a rainy day in an otherwise sunny week, you'll be able to disconnect from the negativity and wait for things to get better again. Choosing to accept (rather than to change) other people leaves room for making relationships more positive, both now and in the future.

It takes a great deal of inner strength to recognize how you can remain positive and present in the midst of a relationship's storm. Here are some tactics to help you embrace an accepting nature in a relationship you're currently struggling with but which you know you want to continue to nurture.

BEHIND
EVERY *cloud*...

...IS A *blue sky*

1. FOCUS ON THE POSITIVE

A positive mental state is yours for the taking. You don't need to feed off anyone else's positivity, because you can create your own. Tune in to the positive interactions you still share within your relationship and notice how these make you feel. For example, your friend might be driving you crazy with her incessant complaining, but she still makes you laugh with her silly antics. Directing your attention to positive interactions that are still happening (or to those that have happened and you know will happen again) will help you maintain a positive inner state.

reminder!
POSITIVELY PRESENT PRINCIPLE #1

Open your mind to being positive and present by focusing on good experiences you've had as a couple in the past. Just as it helps to remind yourself that the sun will shine again after a storm, this is a useful way of combatting a relationship's negative state when times are tough.

2. FIND EXTERNAL SUPPORT

If you're struggling to understand someone you love or having trouble dealing with their actions, ask a close friend (or see an impartial therapist) for advice. Simply sharing what you're going through can provide a fresh, enlightening perspective on the situation, and with better understanding comes a greater ability to accept. In addition, airing your emotional state to someone removed from the relationship can prevent you from sharing negative thoughts and feelings with the person you're struggling to get along with, which may cut down on the amount of negative interactions you experience.

3. KNOW YOU'RE OFTEN POWERLESS OVER OTHERS

No matter how much you might care about someone – or how much time you spend together – you cannot control what other people think, say or do. When you accept your powerlessness over others, you begin to free yourself from the mental anguish that goes along with wanting to change them, even if you truly believe changes would make them "better". You will find your way back to each other more quickly if you're both able to stay focused on what each of you have control over internally and don't attempt to control one another.

4. FIND THE SILVER LINING

This is a relationship you've chosen to keep working on, which means that somewhere in the cloud of negativity must lie a silver lining. Focus on one positive aspect of your relationship – for example, how your sister is a great listener, how your best friend makes you laugh, how your lifelong friend always offers to have your kids when you're busy. Hold this positive thought like the precious gift that it is and keep it with you even when the relationship seems frosty or uncommunicative. It's much easier to make it through the storm when you keep in mind that, behind the clouds, there is still a blue sky.

5. RECOGNIZE YOUR OWN WEAKNESSES

As the saying goes, it takes two to tango. Your own behaviour and reactions within a relationship – especially to the things the other person is doing or saying – have an impact on the harmony between you, too. Try to counter situations in which you're likely to get angry or upset by pausing before you react and turning your responses on their head. If you feel like shouting, respond quietly; if you want to storm out and slam a door, sit down and hug a cushion instead. Also try to recognize when your own behaviour causes the other person to bristle. If possible, work together to find ways to give each other space and be respectful of each other's needs. We all have weaknesses and it's important to recognize and accommodate them (and even to be ready to apologize for them) in order to get a relationship back on track.

APPLY IT!
list your no-go life traits

Make a list of at least ten personality traits, habits or lifestyle choices found in other people that you know would have a negative impact on your life. This list will be very personal to you: something you find detrimental to your emotional health, such as other people making judgmental comments, might not bother someone else so much. Then watch out for these traits and steer clear of people who will not suit you well. In existing relationships, you can focus on ways to work around your no-go traits.

LEARNING TO *Say no*

N o is a powerful word when it comes to relationships. Too much of it isn't a good thing (who wants to be always on the receiving end of endless negativity?), but not enough of it isn't good either. Consider the times when "yes" was your default response without first contemplating whether or not saying yes would actually have a positive impact on your life. You've probably encountered situations when you realized days – or perhaps even just hours – later that "no" would really have been the better option, even if it would have been the more difficult word to say.

There are all sorts of reasons why saying no, negative as it sounds, can be a more positive response. For example, it might save you from having to spend time with people who bring negativity into your life; or it might ensure you don't overload your schedule. It can also strengthen relationships because it lets other people know you have boundaries and will enforce them. It helps others know where they stand – and if they don't cross the line, your relationship is all the more positive for it.

As beneficial as saying no can sometimes be, it's not always easy – particularly for those of us who tend to put the needs of others before our own. But saying no when you need to shows respect for yourself, and this respect circles back to you in your relationships. Here are some of the best ways to master the art of declining gracefully.

1. VALUE YOUR OWN TIME
How often do you hear yourself say, "I wish I had more time ..."? More often than you'd like, I bet. Your time is precious and the more you value it, the easier it becomes to say no when demands on your time start to mount up. Try not to feel guilty about saying no to preserve your time and remind yourself that your emotions are greatly influenced by

the amount of time you feel you have. You'll feel stronger, more positive and more able to invest in positive relationships if you have said no when you need to.

2. DON'T BE AFRAID TO USE THE WORD "NO" ITSELF

"No" has such negative connotations that sometimes we're afraid to actually say it. Instead, we say things like "I'll have to think about it ..." or "I'm not sure, maybe ..." This may not only confuse others (is that a yes or a no?), but may also dilute your own thoughts – and resolve – as well. Do your best to embrace the word when you're certain you don't want to (or don't have time to) engage in a particular activity or do something with a particular person.

3. LEAVE OUT EXCUSES AND EXPLANATIONS

When you turn down a request or an invitation, it's tempting to want to provide a reason for doing so. However, explanations often sound less convincing than you hope them to be. Your reasons are yours alone and others don't necessarily need to know them. If you're asked for a reason, be as truthful as you can without being hurtful. Good relationships are built on honest interactions and you'll feel worse about saying no if you feel you've had to finish off with a lie or half-truth.

reminder!
POSITIVELY PRESENT PRINCIPLE #4

Love and appreciate who you are by saying no, whether that's to give yourself time, to stand up for yourself or to value your own feelings. Saying no is not selfish; it's how you make sure *your* needs are important, too.

4. STAND YOUR GROUND

Have you ever met someone who won't take no for an answer? You know the type – the ones who pepper you with questions or try to come up with creative solutions to make it possible for you to say yes. When you encounter this type of person, stand your ground and simply repeat your initial response. (If you find yourself wanting to waiver, remind yourself of the reasons you chose to say no in the first place, and hold firm.)

5. REALIZE "NO" CAN MEAN "YES"

That sounds confusing, I know, but consider this: when you say no to something that has the potential to be negative for you, you're indirectly saying yes to spending your time doing something else, something likely to be a much more positive experience. If you're struggling to say no, imagine exactly what you would do with the time you free up if you do so. Envisioning a more positive or productive way to spend your time is a great way to empower yourself to say no.

APPLY IT!
just say no

Practise saying no this week. The next time you are asked to do something that doesn't interest you or that may bring more negativity and stress into your life, just say no. If you don't think that simple response will suffice, below are some ways to say no politely, but firmly and clearly.

- "I'd love to, but no thank you, I can't." (No explanation needed!)
- "I'd love to help you out, but I have too many other commitments right now, so I have to say no this time."
- "No, unfortunately, I won't be able to make it."
- "That sounds like a wonderful opportunity, but no unfortunately I won't be able to attend."
- "No, it doesn't work for me right now, but do ask again."
- "Thank you for thinking of me, but I'm going to have to say no at this time."
- "I understand how you feel, but no I don't think I'm the right person to help you out."
- "I don't have any experience with that so no, it's not a great fit for me."
- "No, I can't help you with X, but I'll be happy to do Y."

COMPARING LESS, *loving more*

N o matter how much you love who you are – and if you're still working on that, as most of us are, check out the section on self-love (see pages 132–9) – it's pretty hard not to compare yourself to others. As you probably know, comparison, and the potential for jealousy that inevitably comes with it, are nothing but negative influences on your relationships. When we compare ourselves to others, we focus our attention on what we wish we had, rather than what we already have. All around us are messages that encourage us to make sure we look the best, have the best stuff and feel better than everyone else. But making such comparisons is a form of competition and even if you find yourself coming out the "winner", that kind of victory is an unsatisfactory high. Does it really matter that your television set has state-of-the-art 3D functionality while your neighbour's has only 2D? Regardless of what you see others doing, owning or being, you can never truly know how those things or experiences make others feel – nor can you assume how they would make you feel. What is "better" in comparison is always a matter of personal opinion.

Though we might be aware of this, we might still find the urge to compare. Why? For the most part, we compare ourselves to others because we feel insecure or unhappy about the person we are. We're looking to others to see how we measure up. For example, we might critique another's appearance when we're not feeling so great about the way we look; we might put down a person in authority because we ourselves feel helpless; or we might judge another's artistic ability because we don't believe in our own talent.

Regardless of why we make comparisons, what actually is the result of making them? Quite simply: negative feelings, reactions and behaviours. Comparing yourself to someone else is likely to make you feel more, not less insecure; looking for weaknesses in others usually serves only to highlight the weaknesses in yourself. Furthermore, this

APPRECIATE WHAT YOU have

negativity can start to spiral because your comparisons are unlikely to provide you with the reassurance you're seeking, potentially causing you to keep seeking such assurance in the form of further comparisons. Looking from the other person's perspective, you may also cause offence (and doing so will make you feel worse about yourself). Finally, as this negativity whirls around in your life, it becomes increasingly difficult to create positive relationships with others.

But all is not lost! Here are my words of wisdom for putting an end to this cycle of negativity, loving all that is unique and good about you and appreciating what's special about others. If you can put these five steps into practice, you'll build stronger, more positive and more present relationships – not only with others but also with yourself.

1. MONITOR YOUR THOUGHTS

One of the best ways to avoid comparing yourself to others is to become more aware of your own thoughts. That way, when a comparison starts to form, you can stop it in its tracks. Spend ten minutes every day consciously "watching" your thoughts. See them move across the screen of your mind, like subtitles in the cinema. If something negative

reminder!
POSITIVELY PRESENT PRINCIPLE #2

Be aware of – and willing to shift – your thoughts, tuning into which ones are negative and which are positive, and monitoring them particularly for negative comparisons about yourself in relation to others. Challenge negative thoughts with positive outlooks on and assessments of the world and the people around you.

pops into your head, or you start to make a comparison, say "Stop!" to yourself (or use any other word that stops you in your tracks) and make an effort to turn your negative thoughts into positive ones. With practice, you'll begin to watch your thoughts more and more, until doing so becomes instinctive.

2. ACCEPT OTHERS

We are all unique, and our quirks and funny ways make us who we are. Accepting people for who they are is a good first step to accepting yourself. When you push thoughts about others in a positive direction, you'll habitually begin to do the same when you think about yourself. Always try to find something kind to say (or think) about others and give yourself this level of respect and appreciation, too.

3. AVOID STEREOTYPING

Stereotypes are never a positive thing, as they ignore our uniqueness and assume we all fit into categories that are based on concepts of what *should be* rather than what *is*. Appreciate the people around you for who they are, celebrate their differences and interact without pigeonholing. In doing so, you'll start to appreciate, respect and even love uniqueness in yourself as well as others.

4. STOP JUDGING YOURSELF

Sometimes your inner critic inspires you to become better, but most of the time it forces you to be hard on yourself. The less you judge yourself (the way you look, the stuff you have, the way you smile/laugh/chat), the less likely you are to compare yourself to others.

PAY ATTENTION TO
what is,
NOT WHAT COULD BE

5. SEE IT FROM THE OTHER PERSPECTIVE

If you're still struggling to stop comparing yourself to others, put yourself in the shoes of the person you're comparing yourself to. Think about how you feel when someone compares themselves to you – does it feel like you're being judged or scrutinized somehow? How uncomfortable does it make you feel? Consider how living positively shouldn't really involve making people feel awkward or inferior in this way. Now switch your thinking and remember how it feels when you know someone has seen the positive in you. You want to feel that way, and make others feel that way.

APPLY IT!
use positive language

It's pretty hard to criticize and compare if you focus on using positive words to describe the world. Each day, try to use at least three words from the list below. Every time a negative phrase floats into your mind, challenge it with one of these words. Check out danidipirro.com/books/guide for a longer list.

- Awesome
- Beautiful
- Cheerful
- Dazzling
- Empowering
- Fearless
- Genuine
- Hopeful
- Insightful
- Jovial
- Kindhearted
- Loving
- Motivated
- Noteworthy
- Optimistic
- Peaceful
- Qualified
- Resourceful
- Serene
- Talented
- Unique
- Visionary
- Wonderful
- Youthful
- Zealous

SAY "QUIET!" TO YOUR INNER CRITIC

(it's just unnecessary static)

CHAPTER FOUR

being positively present in love

A h, love! It's the subject of poetry and much great literature, the source both of happily ever after and of harrowing heartbreak. When you're in the first thrilling throes of love, nothing seems better. But when love ends, as it sometimes must do, you can feel trapped beneath a cloud of sorrow, the world void of any light and happiness. Love is a two-sided coin – both sunshine and shadow. When it's wonderful, it's wonderful. When it's not, well ... it's rough.

Because of its complex nature, romantic love – while not vital to living a meaningful, magnificent life (yes, you can live perfectly well without a romantic partner!) – can have a significant influence on your life. Love (a term I'll use primarily in reference to romantic love in this chapter) has the ability to set your heart aflame with lust, passion and excitement – and also to burn that same heart to a crisp with loss, heartbreak and pain.

While Chapter Three discusses being positively present in non-romantic relationships, this chapter will now explore what I believe to be the essential aspects of romantic love: learning to love yourself, avoiding negativity, creating an exciting love, maintaining a steady love, opening yourself up to love and healing a broken heart. People have been writing about love since time immemorial. I don't claim to have all the answers, but over the years I've learned a thing or two about it – particularly about how we can use love to create a more positive and more present life.

Whether you're falling in love, in the middle of love, or at the mercy of love lost, as you read this chapter, keep in mind that romantic love is only one part of your life. Despite the attention it's typically given in popular culture and the amount of time many of us spend ruminating on it, romantic love is only a portion of the love we have to give and receive. Love, in the general sense of the word, is absolutely essential for making the most of every moment. You benefit a great deal from loving yourself, loving what you do, loving those close to you, and even loving those you don't know at all. You might be wondering why I'm raising this point just as I'm about to launch into an entire chapter dedicated to the subject of romantic love, but a positively present life requires balance and this chapter represents exactly what romantic love should be in a positively present life – a single, amazing chapter in the book of your life.

FALLING IN LOVE, with yourself

L ike anything we need to learn, loving and allowing ourselves to be loved are things we need to practise in order to become good at them. Quite simply, the more you love, the better you become at loving; and the more you let love into your life, the easier it becomes to make the most of all the moments in your life, and to stay positive and present. However, the act of truly, deeply loving others, and embracing their love in return, begins with a single act: falling in love with yourself.

You might have noticed that loving yourself is one of the Positively Present Principles (see pages 18–21), which may have you wondering why I've also dedicated a section to it. I've done so because loving yourself is vital not only to making your whole life more positive and present, but also to creating lasting romantic relationships.

I like to think of relationships as a pyramid. At the bottom of the pyramid lie the foundation stones made up of the love you have for yourself. If these stones are properly laid, cemented together and strong, you create a robust base for other major relationships in your life – those with friends, family and so on – creating a solid middle section for the pyramid. At the top of the pyramid, in the most precarious position, sits your relationship with your significant other – your romantic relationship. If your foundation stones are cracked or badly placed, your romantic relationship can wobble and waver and is the part of the pyramid most likely to topple over. Don't believe me? See page 134 for three key ways in which loving yourself impacts romantic love.

reminder!
POSITIVELY PRESENT PRINCIPLE #4

Loving and appreciating yourself is imperative not only for living a positive and present life, but also when it comes to romantic relationships. Loving yourself is the first step down the path to successful, lasting romance.

BE ~~WITH~~
SOMEONE WHO
MAKES YOU
happy

loving YOURSELF MAKES you ....

... less critical of others. As you probably know, criticism can be a deadly thorn in even the most loving relationship. However, it's often the traits you don't love in yourself that bother you in others. When you love yourself, you don't feel the need to make harsh judgments about other people.

... less likely to settle for an unfulfilling relationship. When you love and respect yourself, you value yourself too much to settle for a relationship that doesn't boost your confidence or inspire you. The feeling of having settled will eventually breed resentment -- and resentment is deadly to romance.

... more likely to gravitate toward things and people that bring positivity into your life. This is because, as I'm sure you've heard, like attracts like. The more you focus on the positives within yourself, the more you'll seek out and notice positives in others, increasing your chances of finding a great match or enhancing your current relationship.

You might think loving yourself sounds easy, but is it? Sometimes self-love is associated with being self-indulgent or selfish. In fact, loving yourself is just the opposite: a selfless act. The more you love yourself, the more that love will transfer to those around you. Unfortunately, sometimes we are our own worst critics, creating obstacles in the path of self-love. As you may already know, there will be moments when self-love seems like an impossible goal. But then all the best things in life need striving for, and the important thing to remember is that you have the power to take the first step in the cycle of love.

If you're not familiar with the cycle of love – which you're probably not, as it's my own little invention – it's the notion that if you love yourself, you open yourself up to being loved by others. When you open yourself up to love, you are then capable of loving others. The more you love others, the more you then love yourself, thus completing the cycle of love!

Below are some techniques to help you master the delicate art of loving who you are.

1. PAY ATTENTION TO THOUGHTS ABOUT YOURSELF

Even once you're committed to loving yourself, it takes enormous amounts of self-confidence and self-belief to pursue that love when there may be a negative voice in your head chiming in occasionally (or often!). How can you love yourself, for example, when you look in the mirror and see only what you wish you could change? How can you love yourself when you're ruminating on mistakes you've made in the past? No matter what negative mutterings you hear in your head (we all have them!), shout over them with the belief that you are worthy of your own love. The voice of self-doubt is so subtle that sometimes you don't even realize it's there. More worryingly, sometimes it becomes such a part of your thinking patterns that you may hesitate to suppress it for fear of who you'll become without it there to hold you back. Pay attention to how you think about yourself. Really listen to thoughts forming in your mind and ask yourself, "Is this how I would think about someone else?" Your thoughts about yourself are often much more critical than those you have about others. Paying attention to your thoughts – and being willing to question those that are negative – is an essential first step to embracing self-love.

celebrate yourself

THE WAY YOU WOULD
CELEBRATE A FRIEND

2. ACCEPT YOUR CHOICES

Everyone makes good choices – and everyone makes bad ones. Some are big and important; others are minor and barely significant. Regardless of whether you've labelled your decisions good or bad, accept them. They are done. You don't have to *love* them, but you do have to *live with* them. You can't go back and undo what you've done; you can only make the most of the moment you are in right now. Through acceptance of both the good and the bad, you show yourself love.

3. LEARN FROM YOUR MISTAKES

You might not always make the right choices, say the right things or do exactly what you should. But that's OK. Don't beat yourself up over mistakes you've made; instead, think of them as opportunities to learn and grow, to do things right the next time. (This might sound clichéd, but it really is true!) Some say the more you live, the more you learn, and I think that's because the more you live, the more mistakes you make! (And sometimes you have to make the same mistake more than once: like when you have to go out with at least three touring musicians before you realize that dating someone who is always travelling doesn't mesh well with your homebody preferences!) However hard they are to find, there are always life lessons amid the rubble of bad decisions. Love yourself not by ruminating on what went wrong, but by learning what you can and moving on.

4. APPRECIATE YOUR FLAWS

When it comes to loving other people, you inevitably overlook flaws and focus on the good bits. But I bet you aren't that easy on yourself. We all tend to be a bit (or a lot!) harder on ourselves than we are on others. Sometimes self-criticism can be a good thing, a driving force to move you in a more positive direction, but quite frequently it's simply a roadblock. Your flaws are as much a part of the tapestry of you as your best qualities, so try to love and embrace your imperfections – physical, mental and, yes, even emotional.

5. TREAT YOURSELF AS A FRIEND

How often do you do something nice for yourself for no other reason than to show yourself a little love? You probably don't do things just for you all that often, but you should! A small act of kindness is such a great way to show someone else love, and it's just as rewarding to do something kind for yourself. Treat yourself as you would a dear friend. Show yourself compassion when you've had a hard day. Pick up a little treat for yourself "just because". Cook yourself your favourite meal because a meeting went well. Keeping an eye out for excuses to treat yourself well will help you focus on how worthy you are of love and give you an opportunity to celebrate yourself in the present.

6. SING YOUR OWN PRAISES

Learn to treat your accomplishments the way you would someone else's. Celebrate when you reach a milestone. Get excited when you overcome an obstacle. Tell others about what you've done. The more you acknowledge your successes, the more you'll remind yourself of your own unique skills and talents. Of course no one wants to be around a Boastful Betty, but people do want to be around those who are confident and excited about the great things they've done. Singing your own praises not only draws others to you, but it reminds you that you are worthy of positive and present moments.

APPLY IT!
make an "I love me!" list

Write down 20 things you love about yourself, each one on a different scrap of paper or sticky note. Place those 20 pieces of paper randomly around your home, office and car, to serve as reminders of how fantastic you are. Every time you feel yourself having doubts about your own greatness, find one of those notes and read it to remind yourself of a solid reason that you are deserving of your own love.

YOU ARE MORE THAN WHAT YOU SEE IN THE MIRROR

7. LEARN TO LOOK PAST THE MIRROR

How closely is your self-worth tied to what you see in the mirror? If your appearance is tightly knotted to how you feel about yourself, say aloud these words right now: "I am more than what I look like." Even if you love the way you look – and I hope you do! – it's important to remember that you are more than just your outward appearance. Besides, the person you see in the mirror isn't necessarily the person the rest of the world sees. We all look at ourselves through spectacles dirtied by years of staring at and critiquing the same image. You are more than just your reflection. You are your thoughts and your ideas and your mindset and your skills and your heart and your spirit and your passion. You are your goals and your dreams and your past and your present and your future. You are a culmination of all the moments you've lived until now. So, never forget that you are so much more than muscle and skin and bone.

BATTING AWAY *negativity*

I n an ideal world every moment of a romantic relationship would be filled with only happy, loving, positive interactions. However, when two people come together – even two people who love one another very much – there are bound to be areas of conflict. No two people are so alike that they agree on *everything*. Conflict itself isn't necessarily a bad thing – just as long as you don't allow it to dominate your relationship. In other words negativity itself is not necessarily a problem as long as you know how to minimize its impact.

Potentially negative situations – differing opinions, conflicts of interest, opposite draws on your time, to name a few – are simply balls of energy waiting to be transformed.

APPLY IT!
write a letter you'll never send

Sometimes, when you face a negative situation, it's best to work through your thoughts and to articulate them without necessarily throwing them out into the relationship – at least until you're sure something good or worthwhile will come of them. If you have a lot to say about a situation or characteristic of your relationship, try writing a letter to your partner, expressing how you feel. Be full and frank in your statements and explanations. Then, when you've finished, destroy the letter – delete it from your computer, rip it up into tiny pieces and throw it away – and never hand it over to your partner. Getting your thoughts out of your head and into a neutral space is often enough to relieve you of your negativity and allow yourself to revisit your relationship in a more positive frame of mind.

If you can transform them into something useful and potentially positive, you can prevent negative emotions, actions or words from infiltrating your relationship. Here are my tips on how to harness the positive energy in disagreement and turn it into something that brings you together, rather than drives you apart.

1. AVOID RIGHT/WRONG DICHOTOMIES

In the heat of an argument, of course you are right and your partner is wrong! *Of course*, you are! The only problem is, your "right" is often the exact opposite of your partner's "right". When you feel the right/wrong dichotomy approaching, try to stop, take a breath and start over with the points on which you agree, then work outward into the more unstable territory. You might think you don't agree about anything, but I bet there are plenty of grey areas where each of you is a bit right and a bit wrong and can agree to disagree. Remember that sometimes it's OK to agree to disagree, and sometimes letting someone else be right is the "right" thing to do.

2. REVERSE YOUR PERSPECTIVE

In the midst of a negative interaction, it's hard not to think only about your own perspective, but try your best to be empathetic. Consider how you would feel or react if the situation were reversed. Putting yourself in your partner's shoes might not solve the problem completely, but it will at least allow you to consider different possible solutions. And you might be surprised by how you feel (and react) when you imagine yourself on the other side of an argument. The more you step away from rehashing what you believe to be right, the more likely you'll be to come to a more positive resolution to your conflict.

3. LOOK AT WHAT'S HAPPENING RIGHT NOW

Conflict is frequently a consequence of not staying in the moment. You'll probably find yourself facing negative interactions when you're stressed about what has happened or what could potentially happen (you know, the imagined scenarios in which that gorgeous fitness instructor becomes too much of a temptation for your partner). When you find yourself in a negative place, take a deep breath and bring yourself back to the moment,

BEFORE YOU SPEAK, ARE YOU REALLY *listening?*

asking yourself, "What's really happening *right now*?" Redirecting your attention to the moment helps you focus on what *is*, rather than what *was* or what *could be*. Keep it positive by focusing only on the present.

4. ASK THOUGHTFULLY AND LISTEN CAREFULLY

It's important to keep the lines of communication open in your relationship (for more on this, check out pages 98–103). When you're not completely certain how your partner feels, ask. And, more importantly, really listen to the answers instead of hearing what you *think* will be said, or carving out your response in your head before you've heard everything your partner has to say. The more you ask – and listen – the more knowledge you'll have, and the more likely you'll be to understand your partner's perspective.

5. PRACTISE GIVE AND TAKE

All relationships – and particularly romantic ones – benefit from a little give and take. To keep positivity at the forefront of a relationship, it's important to be willing to give love, time and energy – and also to be willing to accept what's being given to you by your significant other. In positive relationships both partners need to feel that they contribute love, support and comfort to the life of the other. To avoid unnecessary negativity in your relationship, be ready to give *and* to receive.

6. BE GRACIOUSLY GRATEFUL

A good relationship needs gratitude. When you spend a significant amount of time with someone – particularly if you live with that person – it's so easy to forget to be thankful for them, even when your love is very strong. Make a continual conscious effort to let your partner know how much you value them and the relationship you have. You don't have to spend money or even time showing your gratitude – a squeezed hand, an unsolicited "I love you", a note on a pillow can be enough. It's the little things that count.

reminder!
POSITIVELY PRESENT PRINCIPLE #5

Adopting an attitude of gratitude for the people in your life is one of the best ways to stay positive and present. Pay attention to the ways your partner makes your life better and make a point actually to say the words: "thank you".

7. HAVE A FORGIVING HEART

No relationship is perfect, because no *person* is perfect. At times, one of you will do or say things that do the exact opposite of promoting a positive and present situation. It might be tempting to dwell on these flaws and missteps, but doing so only draws attention to the negative and gives it power. Instead, cultivate a forgiving heart (for yourself as well as for your partner) and in doing so re-anchor yourself in the current moment – a moment filled with potential for promoting positivity in your relationship.

KEEPING THE BUTTERFLIES *fluttering*

f you've been in love, you'll know how those first, thrilling moments of meeting someone can feel – the quickening of your heart, the butterflies fluttering in your stomach. If you've had a lasting relationship, you'll probably also know how those first, heady feelings are quite different from the day-to-day existence of ongoing love. For some, butterflies-in-the-stomach lasts for a long time (although I've read that, at most, it's a couple of years); for others, it fades quickly. What's left is often more substantial – perhaps even more meaningful – but sometimes it can feel a little bit mundane. When you've reached that stage in your relationship, it's good to try to get back into the moment of the first flush of love, to recreate that fluttering butterflies feeling.

I've been in enough relationships to know those butterflies aren't easy to come by day in, day out. Keeping that feeling alive takes work – like anything that's truly worthwhile. Even so, there are lots of really positive steps you can take to make sure your relationship is filled with love, excitement and positivity on a day-to-day basis.

1. CHAT – A LOT!

Do we ever really know *everything* about a person? Even the person we share most of our life with? There's always more to discover, no matter how long you've been with someone. Chatting – and that means chit-chat as well as serious conversation – means you'll never lose the habit of finding out about one another. With lines of communication open between you, you increase the odds of thrilling each other with new knowledge, fresh discoveries or solutions to joint problems. The more you share, the more you learn about one another and the closer you'll become – even after many years! As well as surprising you, perhaps even making your heart leap, learning new things about your loved one and maintaining your romantic connection will also make it easier to talk about difficult things when they crop up.

2. MAKE TIME FOR EACH OTHER

Life is busy. With careers, family commitments and social lives, making time for each other often gets pushed to the bottom of the to-do list. But if you want to experience that just-falling-in-love feeling, find ways to spend time together – just the two of you – as often as you can. This might sometimes mean skipping out on other commitments or compromising on group activities in order to spend quality time with one another. Don't assume you'll just happen to find the time to be together – get your calendars out and schedule it! Think about how important it was to make sure you spent time together when you first met, and try not to take the time you have now for granted. Spending time together is as important for your relationship now as it was at the start.

3. DO THE LITTLE (ROMANTIC!) THINGS

At the beginning of a relationship, you and your partner might have spent more time on the little things – sending sweet notes, checking in for no reason with a quick call or an email, or picking up little presents for one another on the way home from the office. As time goes on, we often begin to forget just how meaningful those little tokens of love are. Make today the day to bring them back into your life. Send a quick email that simply reads "I love you." Or pick up your partner's favourite food for dinner. Or tuck a little love note into their jacket pocket. These things might seem silly, but all of these little things can add up to a whole lot of romance.

reminder!
POSITIVELY PRESENT PRINCIPLE #5

Adopt an attitude of gratitude by doing little things for the one you love. You're embracing thankfulness every time you treat the one you love with a hug, a kiss, a touch or a gift. Every small act is a physical manifestation of your gratitude.

4. BE SUPPORTIVE

Think about how it feels when someone is supportive of you. Supportive partners fill your heart with love and appreciation. To be supportive yourself, talk to your significant other about the things that matter most to them. Ask about your partner's work (even

RELEASE THE PAST.
FORGET THE FUTURE.
APPRECIATE THE GIFT
OF THE *present.*

if it might seem a little boring to you). Ask about your partner's favourite pastime. Ask about your partner's thoughts and feelings on current issues. Offer a hug, advice, a statement of unconditional love. There's nothing that makes the heart quicken more than knowing you've got someone to watch your back no matter what.

5. SET ASIDE THE PAST AND THE FUTURE

A stomach filled with butterflies is all about the present – or at least the near-present. It's about the moment you see your partner when they walk into the room or when they take your hand while you are watching TV; or perhaps it's about your anticipation of meeting up after work or about a memory of a recent moment of closeness. Day to day, try not to spend all your time worrying about something that happened in the past or that might happen in the future. Instead, focus on what's happening right now in your relationship. If there are other, non-immediate matters to discuss, schedule a specific time to discuss them.

APPLY IT!
recreate a date

Remember the first date you went on with your loved one? At some point in the near future, strive to recreate that date. Go back to the same restaurant (or if it's no longer around, somewhere that serves similar cuisine) or return to the spot of your first kiss. Although it might seem backward-looking, recreating a positive past memory with the one you love can be a wonderful way to celebrate the present you have together, especially if you make a point to reflect on all the things you now share that you didn't back when you first met.

MAINTAINING YOUR HAPPILY *ever after*

veryone loves the idea of happily ever after, of embarking on a path of love that they hope will last for ever. But whether you had to overcome obstacles to be together or your eyes fatefully met across a crowded room, what happens after that first momentary flush of love? How do you get from that to a kind of love that's even more beautiful (if less flashy): a long-lasting, true love that can withstand the (many!) tests of time?

Being with someone for ever means you will face a lot of challenges together, both as individuals and together, within your relationship. Ideally, these challenges – and the process of overcoming them together – add value to your relationship, making it more robust. But that's possible only if you can keep showing each other how much love you have between you. You might do it with flowers or kisses, or you might find kind words or supportive acts – but most significantly you can continue to show your love through the way you interact with one another.

There are a myriad of wonderful ways in which to show love in a relationship, but I think four are particularly effective. As a bonus, I've given them a particularly memorable acronym – L.O.V.E. Visit danidipirro.com/books/guide for a free download that you can print out to keep these aspects of showing love in mind.

LAUGHTER

It is said that laughter is the best medicine – and I believe laughter is one of the best ways to keep your relationship healthy. When you laugh, you feel good; when you hear other people laughing, you also feel good. So when you laugh with those you love, you create good feeling between the two of you. The more positive interactions you have, the stronger your relationship becomes, and shared laughter is one of the most

WHATEVER YOU DO,
DO IT WITH
love

important positive interactions out there. Of course, this counts only if the laughter is filled with joy and positivity, rather than being malicious or spiteful, so try to encourage laughter in a positive way (for example, while watching a funny TV programme or sharing stories, not while mocking your socially awkward cousin!).

Opportunities

An opportunity can be transforming – it can change a whole life. And although it might not seem the most romantic way to demonstrate your love, offering your partner opportunities – perhaps to do something they love but you don't care much for, or

WHAT wisdom
CAN YOU SHARE
WITH OTHERS?

even to pursue a new career by carrying the financial burden for a while (among myriad other possibilities) – opens your heart and expresses your love. Another opportunity you could offer your loved one is a chance to get to know more about you – sharing more of yourself will bring them closer to you and facilitate a stronger bond in your relationship.

reminder!
POSITIVELY PRESENT PRINCIPLE #2

Be aware of – and willing to shift your thoughts – by sharing and listening to enlightened ideas with the one you love. You may discover new ways of thinking about the world or about your relationship, so strive to keep an open mind and heart throughout your sharing.

VALIDATION

Most people – whether they'll admit it or not – seek some sort of validation to confirm they are worthy of love and support. Validating someone's actions – and even their existence – is a superb way to show love. This might be in the form of those three little words – "I love you" – or it could be in a more tangible way, such as highlighting your partner's strengths to other people or listening attentively to what your partner has to say. Validation expresses your love on a deeper level. It says, "You matter. You count. You are important to me."

ENLIGHTENMENT

Offering what you know to those you love creates new pathways of openness, understanding and shared knowledge. When someone you love shares information with you – especially information that makes you feel more enlightened about yourself and the world – that is an act of love in itself. When someone enlightens you in some way, you feel more connected to and inspired by them. When you transform someone else's view of the world, whether that's through a great life lesson or by giving them a simple trick for making supper more efficiently, that act of love continues to create your own happily ever after.

UNLOCKING YOUR HEART *to love*

Another important step on the road to romantic relationship success is to find that special one – or at least to be mindful about, and open to, finding them. So many people are afraid to open their hearts to love. Perhaps you've had a broken heart that has scared you into locking the door and throwing away the key, or perhaps you've had difficulty even opening the door in the first place. Believe it or not, there are ways to develop confidence in love and your ability to be loved that may help you open up again. Or, perhaps you think you've been open to love, but it simply hasn't found you yet. If that sounds like you, this is a good place to get started, too; you'll find inspiration for keeping your heart and mind open to new possibilities.

If you're the type of person who tends to be emotionally closed off (whatever the reason), you're probably focused on how to keep people out, rather than on letting them in. Keeping your heart closed might seem like the ultimate in self-preservation – a way to avoid an onslaught of negative emotions in the future – but locking up your heart prevents you from enjoying so many positive experiences. How can you fully connect in each moment with the relationships you already have (that is, the non-romantic ones) if your heart is closed? How can you form strong, positive relationships if you push people away?

I've always struggled a bit with having an open heart. I've been suspicious and mistrustful of those who want to show me love. It's only when I've consciously acknowledged this and chosen to open my heart (which is usually really scary for me!) that I've discovered meaningful connections. And those meaningful connections have led me to significant relationships and even, in some cases, to love. Had I kept my heart closed, I never would have had so many positive experiences, really making the most of every moment with those around me. Here are some tactics you might want to try if you're struggling to crack open the door to your heart.

OPEN YOUR *heart*
TO OPEN YOUR *mind*

1. BE OPEN TO LEARNING

The more you are open to learning – through your own experiences and the wisdom of others – the more you will know; and the more you know, the more likely you are to relate to others, regardless of age, background or anything else. Knowledge makes you smarter, more creative and more empathetic. It opens your heart in a way that allows you to see the world from new viewpoints, which helps you connect with those around you.

2. MONITOR YOUR NON-VERBAL CUES

Sometimes closing yourself off emotionally manifests itself in physical "symptoms". If you're afraid to smile, if you keep your arms crossed or if you always look down at your toes or over someone's shoulder, you're letting others know you aren't open to the idea of friendship, let alone love. Open your body language – smile, uncross those arms, look people in the eye – and in doing so watch how they respond more positively to you. Allow this to give you confidence in the notion of opening yourself up emotionally and letting someone in. Little by little, as people approach you and respond to you with their own openness, you'll feel more like receiving their attention without suspicion and with an open heart.

reminder!
POSITIVELY PRESENT PRINCIPLE #1

Open your mind to being positive and present by unlocking your heart to love. If you don't at least crack open the door, love can't find a way in.

3. IGNORE YOUR FEAR

In order to live a more positive and present life, it's important to acknowledge rather than ignore negative emotions. However, when it comes to opening your heart to others, setting aside the negative emotion of fear and replacing it with positivity can really help. Think about why you're afraid to open your heart. Are you worried about being judged? Do you fear your openness will be rejected or rebuffed? In order to bask in the light of potential new relationships, you need to step out of the shadow of your fear. One way to do this is to ask yourself, "Will this matter a year from now?" or "What do I really have to lose?" When you consider questions such as these, you're likely to notice that the risk of ignoring your fear is much lower than the potential rewards you might reap from doing so.

4. STAY IN THE MOMENT

When you're hesitating to open your heart, it's usually because of fears connected to the past or concerns about what the future might hold. If you catch yourself agonizing over your relationship history, or fretting about your relationship future, bring yourself back to the present. Shift your attention to what's actually happening in the moment of your interactions – listen attentively, talk openly, drink in the sights and smells around you. If you find your mind drifting off to the past or the future, reconnect with the present again – and keep reminding yourself to do so as often as is needed. If you concentrate on the positive things happening right now, you are more likely to open your heart to the moment's potential – and the potential of a relationship.

5. STOP JUDGING

No one likes to be judged. Considering what others might think about us can be intimidating, sometimes so much so that (imagined) opinions can hold us back from creating interpersonal connections. You might think the way to avoid judgment is just to keep the door to your heart firmly closed. But consider this concept – you get what you give. If you appear open, receptive and accepting of others just as they are, that's exactly how people will see you. Try not to worry about how other people view you, and especially try to avoid making assessments about others based on your own preconceived ideas or previous experiences. The more open-minded you are about other people, the more open-minded other people will be about you.

6. BE SPECIFIC

When you're trying to connect with others, particularly those you don't know well, be specific in what you say. When someone says to you, "How was your day?" don't respond with, "Fine. Yours?" Try to be more specific. Give details. Provide examples. Share stories. People will feel more connected to you (and will probably share some of their own stories) if you open up to them with specifics. You can also do some specific asking with creative questions, such as "What's your favourite colour? Why?" or "I love [insert favourite book or movie here]. Have you seen/read it?"

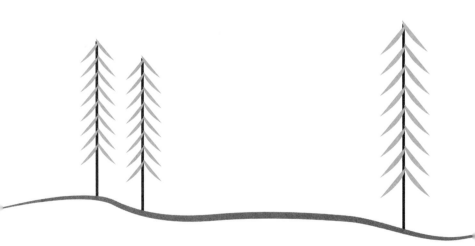

TAKE *love* AT YOUR OWN PACE

7. TAKE YOUR TIME

Opening the door to your heart, especially when openness doesn't come naturally to you, will take time. At first you'll make a single turn of the handle, letting in only a fraction of light. As you develop confidence in how people respond to you when you give a little, you'll open up a tiny bit more. At first you might stumble over your words as you try to answer questions more honestly and creatively. It might take you a while to articulate what you want to say in just the way you want to say it. Be patient with yourself, and don't let a few initially awkward encounters put you off trying again (and again and again if you need to!). The more you practise opening up to others, the easier the process of opening your heart's door will become.

APPLY IT!
share a secret

If you want to develop a closer relationship with someone, share a secret. It doesn't have to be your deepest, darkest secret – in fact, it can be completely trivial – but make sure it's personal, interesting and something you've never told anyone else before. When you experience the release of sharing one small part of yourself, you are one step closer to being able to share your heart.

HEALING A *broken heart*

P erhaps one of the greatest challenges to remaining positive and present is dealing with a broken heart. After all, by definition you didn't choose this particular "now" – your heart is broken because you want something or someone that you don't now have. Focusing on the present probably sounds like the last thing you want to do. To stay positive and present at such a time is more than just a challenge – it might feel like a strenuous battle against the fiercest of foes.

Contrary to how it might seem, staying positive and present is actually one of the best ways to heal your broken heart. When you stay in the moment, you're not focusing on what was happening in the past (the relationship that once was), nor are you pondering the future (wondering what your future relationship status will be and with whom), both of which can make heartache particularly difficult. Just like staying present, staying positive is immensely difficult but vital because it combats the negativity that often comes with heartbreak.

You might be afraid to let go of your sadness. You might fear that if you let it go and move forward, you take an active part in closing a door you may not have wanted to close. You might reason that you don't want to become an accomplice in your broken heart. As a result, sadness becomes something of a habit, something you don't want to let go of because it's oddly comforting (even if it's not helping

reminder!
POSITIVELY PRESENT PRINCIPLE #2

Be aware of – and willing to shift – your thoughts if you're suffering from heartbreak. As soon as you're open to the idea of healing, the process of stitching your heart back together can begin. It can be difficult to let your unhappiness go, but the sooner you open your mind to a new way of thinking, the sooner you'll be able to open your heart.

you stay positive or present). However, letting go of the heartache is the only way you'll be able to move away from the past and into a more positive present, a place where you'll be open to finding someone else to fill your heart with love. Letting go is never easy, but here are some ways you can begin healing your broken heart.

1. MAKE PEACE WITH YOUR PAIN

Although it might be tempting to do so, denying the pain you feel won't help you to make positive progress. Instead, try to accept it and make peace with how you feel by considering the reasons why your relationship didn't work out. Try your best not to apportion blame; just think about where things might have gone wrong, and try to understand why any wrong turns make the experience of the break-up so painful. Spend time with your pain. Take time alone to pay attention to how it actually makes you feel and experience it fully. The amount of time this takes will vary from person to person, but if you allow yourself to fully experience how you are feeling and stay present with your emotions, you'll have a better sense of when you're ready to move forward to a place where you can let go of the pain, allowing yourself a chance to be fully present in a future relationship.

2. KNOW YOU CAN'T REPLACE SOMEONE

Each of us is unique, so it's true that no one else can directly take the place of the person you've just lost. However, there are plenty of other unique individuals in the world, and one of them is much better suited to you. It's a great step on the path to healing a broken heart to remind yourself that you shouldn't pursue a copy of the person you've lost. It's important to seek someone altogether fresh and exciting, and be open to the idea of experiencing something new.

3. THINK OF THE POSITIVES

It's tough to seek out the positives when you're suffering from a broken heart, but I urge you to try. The loss of a relationship that wasn't working is for the best. If someone brought you down more than up, you're better off without this person in your life. If someone ended a relationship with you (whether or not you saw that end coming), tell yourself you don't want to be with someone who doesn't feel the same way you do (trust me, you really don't!). Loss of a negative relationship frees up room in your heart for those positive people who deserve to be there. Recognizing that your heart now has more space to welcome those you love (or new loves!) can be really helpful to promote healing thoughts.

4. DO SOMETHING YOU'VE NEVER DONE BEFORE

The end of one thing is also the start of something else – and that means new discoveries. If you have a broken heart, try something you've never done before. It can be as simple as walking down a street you've always walked right past, or it can be as elaborate as planning a month-long trip to a new and exciting location. Breaking out of your comfort zone and exploring new activities or places keeps you in the moment. When you are

break out OF YOUR comfort zo

immersed in the sights, sounds or experiences of something or somewhere new, you're tuned in to the present, and that means you are tuned out of day dreams about what was or what might have been.

5. FORM NEW BONDS

It's a cliché, but there really *are* "plenty of fish in the sea" – if you're willing to venture into unexplored oceans. Your new beginning has so much to teach you. Consider joining a club or group that focuses on something you're really passionate about (where better to meet someone like-minded?). Or, join your local sports team or walking group. Don't bury yourself in your smartphone – look up, look out and smile! If someone invites you for coffee, accept! It's just coffee ... but who knows where it may lead? At the very least, accepting invitations to bond with others will remind you that others enjoy your company, a confidence boost that can help to heal your broken heart.

APPLY IT!
know what you do (and don't) want

Your broken heart makes a wonderful mirror to reflect what you do and don't want in future relationships. Thinking about what went wrong and what was wonderful about your last relationship can help you to prioritize what you're looking for in someone new. Make a list of what you loved and what you can live without and keep it somewhere safe. Remember that your pain will fade, as will your memory of what went wrong, so it's useful to keep the list to refer to when you're ready to find love again. (Although don't get too hung up ticking off the details to find someone new – sometimes love appears in unexpected places.) Visit danidipirro.com/books/guide to download a worksheet to help you think things through.

CHAPTER FIVE

being positively present during change

hange. It's a scary word, a thrilling word, a word loaded with connotations – both good and bad. Often, we're afraid of it – after all, it's perfectly natural to fear or to be suspicious of what we don't know. In fact, that very instinct has helped to ensure the survival of humankind! It's OK to feel a little afraid of change, but it's *not* OK to let that fear rule your life. When fear holds you back from experiencing new things, you risk encountering something even scarier than change: things always staying as they are.

The thing is, change is unavoidable. Thoughts, actions, places, jobs, children, pets – you name it, everything changes. Sometimes change will happen without your "permission" – you will simply be rolled along with it – and sometimes change will be your choice and you'll be the driving force behind it. Whatever its trigger, change is inevitable, which is why it's important to discover ways to use it to create a more positive, more present life.

WHAT DO YOU WANT TO *change?*

On more than one occasion, change has spun me around, shaken me up, shaped me and transformed me — and time and again it has saved me. I've learned the hard way that change can be my best friend.

Change might make you vulnerable, but it also opens you up to new experiences, allows you to escape something that's not working and inspires you to start again. Above all, change can show you just how strong you can be. When you strive to accept change, embracing it and harnessing it to improve yourself, you are living a positively present life. Change is both freedom and progress.

reminder!
POSITIVELY PRESENT PRINCIPLE #5

Adopt an attitude of gratitude by appreciating change. This is life affirming. Even when change is difficult, be grateful for it. Without it, life would be stagnant and staying present would become increasingly hard.

Of course, when you're facing change you didn't initiate or don't immediately feel like embracing, it can feel anything but liberating, but you can use your thoughts to change how you feel, and try to turn the negatives into positives. You may feel a sense of powerlessness in the face of change — like when you've been let go from a job, when your partner is forced to move across the country or when you don't get accepted to the college of your dreams — but you *do* have power because you have power over your mind, your reactions and your attitude. When you think about it like that, change suddenly becomes a bit less scary.

In this chapter we're going to dig deeper into various types of change and uncover ways to try to keep a positive attitude and stay in the now (no matter what life throws at you!). We'll look first at the most important type of change — the internal one of changing your attitude — and then we'll explore how to deal with unexpected external change, how to turn bad change into good, how to initiate a tough change, how to break bad habits (a particularly tricky type of change!) and how to use change to become the best version of you.

EVERY *change*
YOU FACE

UPGRADES YOU TO
A *better* VERSION OF YOU

CHANGE YOUR ATTITUDE, CHANGE *your life*

When I was a child and I got grumpy about something that was happening, my mum would say to me, "Attitude adjustment!" (or sometimes "AA!" for short). Those two little words used to drive me crazy! But as I got older (like, 20 years older), I realized their wisdom. No matter what the situation, if I changed my attitude, I could make almost anything more manageable. A change in attitude really can change a moment, a situation, even a life. Changing your attitude is the kind of change you have power over at any moment; it allows you to maintain a positive frame of mind no matter what you encounter.

There's also a ripple effect when it comes to choosing a positive attitude: one person's good attitude can cause another's – and another's. Little by little, your positive mindset starts to change the world for the better, and everyone is embracing change.

APPLY IT!
compose a positive mantra

Create a mantra to remind yourself to embrace a positive attitude every time you face a change that doesn't immediately or obviously suit you. It could be something as simple as "I can choose positivity" or as complex as "If I choose a positive attitude at this moment, I will be able to achieve X, Y and Z!" Use your mantra every time you find yourself feeling negative about something that's changing in your life, particularly things over which you have little or no control.

To choose a positive attitude you need to banish negative thoughts – those sneaky little devils that creep into your mind and persist at trying to lead you away from seeing the positive in what's happening around you; unfortunately, once you open the door to one negative thought, a bunch of others seems to creep in. Here are some ways you can keep those pesky negative thoughts at bay when you're faced with unexpected or unwanted change.

reminder!
POSITIVELY PRESENT PRINCIPLE #2

Be aware of – and willing to shift your thoughts from negative to positive, in order to change your attitude. This takes practice and can be tough. You may not change your mind overnight, but don't give up. The more you persevere, the more a new attitude will stick.

1. TAKE CARE OF YOUR BODY

One of the quickest ways to find yourself wandering down the negative-attitude trail is when you're not in a good physical state. If you're exhausted, hungry or stressed, for example, you're going to have a much harder time focusing on the positive aspects of your world and its shifting landscape. Your physical state can have a major impact on how you feel and think, which is why it's essential to take good care of yourself in order to make a positive, present attitude at least a little easier. Enough sleep, healthy foods, a bit of exercise and some fresh air can have a surprisingly big impact on your attitude.

2. LOOK FOR UNDERLYING CAUSES

A negative attitude about a certain situation isn't always as directly tied to that specific scenario as it might seem. When you find your attitude veering into a negative zone, take a closer look at what's truly bothering you. Are you in a negative state of mind because of an argument you had earlier in the day? Are you overly stressed about a situation at work or home? It's tempting to place blame on what's right in front of you, but when you look deeper at the situation, you'll often see something else that *really* needs to be addressed.

3. CONSIDER THE CONSEQUENCES

When you're plagued by a negative attitude (and it happens to all of us, don't worry!), consider how your outlook will impact the situation you're in. For example, let's say you're required to interview a candidate for a job that a close work friend just lost. You feel uncomfortable about the fact that you'll be involved in the new appointment, but will having a negative attitude make the situation any better? Will it help you stay in the moment? Will it allow you to connect with new people and discover new experiences? The answer to those questions is most likely *no*. A negative attitude never improves a situation. When you consider how a negative attitude will make a bad situation worse, you may be able to convince yourself to steer your thoughts in a more positive direction.

4. FOCUS ON SOMEONE ELSE

Negativity is often a result of us being stuck in our own minds, contemplating the ways a situation *should* be instead of allowing it to be what it is. When we find ourselves in a negative mindset, it's helpful to turn attention to other people. Instead of focusing on why *you're* not pleased with the way something's changing, take a look at how others are reacting. You may be surprised that others are finding the positives in ways you might not have considered. And if others are also expressing negative thoughts, challenge yourself to be the positive one (a sort of opposite devil's advocate), to show them a fresh perspective on an apparently negative situation.

5. ASK FOR INPUT

If a negative attitude has become a habit for you (as it was for me for decades!), ask someone close to you to draw your attention gently to your negative comments or reactions as they happen. Just as my mum used to say, "AA!" when I had a negative attitude as a child, you too can have a code word or phrase that a loved one uses to remind you that you're heading into negative territory. Sometimes negative thinking becomes so pervasive that you don't even realize you're doing it. Asking someone you trust to bring you back to the moment can be just the bit of encouragement you need to move your thoughts in a more positive direction.

BE *aware*
OF *YOUR*
thoughts

COPING WITH
unexpected change

There's a proverb that goes, "April showers bring May flowers." I've heard this saying time and again (mostly from my positive-minded mother), but only in recent years did I take the words to heart. The more I think about this phrase, the more I realize how important it is – and how it refers to so much more than storm clouds and blossoms.

It's perfectly normal and natural to feel derailed when a change comes out of nowhere. It's unsettling and even scary to not know quite where a new track might lead. Fear of the unknown can make it hard to envision the possible positivity a change might someday bring. But I believe everything happens for a reason – even when that reason seems out of your grasp, and the only way to find – and benefit from – the reason is to embrace change as best you can. You can bring yourself closer to a more positive, more present life by using the following tactics to cope with change, allowing yourself to discover gradually the ways an unexpected deluge may someday lead to a bouquet of benefits.

reminder!
POSITIVELY PRESENT PRINCIPLE #1

Open your mind to being positive and present by embracing the possibilities of change. However unsettling it is, unexpected change provides an opportunity for growth and transformation so long as you keep your mind and heart open.

1. APPRECIATE A NEW PERSPECTIVE
One of the great benefits of unexpected change is that it offers us a chance to see the world from a new perspective. Think of your new perspective not as something to fear, but as an opportunity to see a situation or person in a new light. Consider how light shifting over the course of a day transforms a landscape – landmarks emerge and recede according to whether they are brightly lit or

cast in shadow. Think also of how the landscape responds to where the light lands over the course of a day: while sunshine brings out blooming flowers, it is in the dark of night that the wise owl emerges. Try always to appreciate the beauty or wonder in the ever-changing landscape of your life, and recognize that changes (no matter how tough they might be) can have positive repercussions.

2. ASSESS YOUR REACTION

Every little change you face, no matter how unexpected, gives you a bit of knowledge about your own ability to cope with change. Faced with sudden change, did you fly into an immediate panic, but sleep on it and wake up with a new sense of calm? Perhaps you took the change well initially, but then found that an insidious anxiety crept up on you later? Perhaps your reaction was far more complex or rollercoaster than either of those scenarios. You may have wanted to talk it through, or you may have wanted to come to terms with it in some other way. Unexpected change gives you an opportunity to

SEEK OUT *beauty* IN TRANSFORMATION

understand better how you relate to change in general. The more you understand about your thoughts, reactions and attitudes, the more you can do to handle unexpected change more efficiently the next time. For example, if you find you'd rather receive news face to face, make sure people know that; likewise, tell them if you prefer to receive such information by email, so you can process it before you have to face anyone. Pay attention to what soothes your worrying mind (a warm bath, a brisk walk, a long run and so on), so you can respond most appropriately to your own needs.

3. PRACTISE ADAPTABILITY

What's the key to human survival? *Adaptability*. Can't imagine how you can cope with your new workload? It will be a matter of considering how to manage your time and prioritize your tasks more efficiently. Even in the face of the worst kind of unexpected change – the loss of a loved one, say – you have an amazing ability to adapt, to draw strength and love from those around you and to arrive stronger on the other side. Whatever you're faced with, give yourself some quiet time when you can consider in what ways you can transform your thinking or support network in order to make your life a little easier during this time of change. Perhaps it means making lists to prioritize your time; or perhaps it means keeping a journal so you're continually working through

APPLY IT!
create the best-case scenario

Instead of pondering all the ways change could be a bad thing, get out some coloured pencils or markers and draw an imaginary scene of what would happen if this change were the best thing ever to happen to you. (If drawing's not your thing, write a list of the good things you imagine this change could bring.) Now that you've envisioned a best-case scenario, focus your mind on making it a reality.

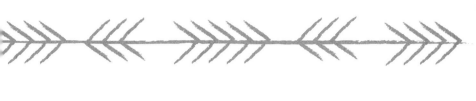

GET OUT OF YOUR OWN WAY

your thoughts and feelings, as well as diarizing how strong you can be. Or, perhaps it means making a more significant change – moving house, changing your lifestyle – in order to adapt to a new situation. Whatever the solution, you can do it.

4. IMAGINE POSSIBILITIES, NOT PROBLEMS

If you must step out of the present and think to the future (and we all must, from time to time), try not to focus on what could go *wrong*, but instead on what could go *right*. Aim yourself in a positive direction by visualizing how this change (however unsettling it may seem right now) just might be a good thing. Spend time daydreaming about all of the ways things could work out well – or at least work out OK. You never know what future might unfurl as a result of just one change so allow yourself to explore it from a positive perspective and let a positive attitude permeate all the consequences of change.

5. CONDUCT A CHANGE REVIEW

For many, change triggers a pattern of emotions: first shock or disbelief, then anger, then sadness and finally acceptance. You may experience some or all of these stages quickly, even in a moment, or they may move through you over a period of time (days, weeks or even years). Whenever you reach the final part of your change journey, contemplate

APPLY IT!
watch your words

When you're worrying about unanticipated change, find a mirror, stand in front of it and recite everything happening right now that scares or concerns you. Try to accept each fear for what it is – not placing any judgment on it – and then imagine your fears being released, simply by speaking them aloud. As the words leave your mouth, imagine that they fly away and can't trouble you any more.

the pattern of your reaction. Did it follow these stages? How did each one manifest itself and how did you cope with it? Now, acknowledge and accept how your life has lost something, perhaps something very precious, as a result of the change. Think about how that loss manifests itself in your life day to day, inwardly and outwardly, but also think about your new beginning or new perspective. What does your review teach you about unexpected change, the transience of its effects and your ability to move through change step by step? Can you acknowledge how your perspective on the change has naturally developed? Keep those lessons in your heart for the next time unexpected change comes your way.

FOCUS ON opportunities NOT OBSTACLES

HANDLING CHANGE ON A *daily basis*

hange is often thought of as "big picture" – the life-altering stuff that rocks your world and sends everything spinning – but in fact we all encounter day-to-day change, too. I'm talking about the little things – your favourite shop not having the tea you prefer in stock, your friend cancelling dinner plans, your schedule suddenly being upended because your boss pops into your office for a chat. Sometimes, these little changes just seem like slightly annoying hiccups in the day, but sometimes they make us feel completely out of control. When you find yourself losing perspective on life's little upsets, try to stay as "in the moment" as you can, keeping as positive and as present an attitude as possible. Here are some tips for doing that.

1. EMBRACE THE UNEXPECTED

Uncertainty helps to make life interesting. Don't panic if a plan changes or things don't work out as you expect. You lose an hour talking to your boss rather than making headway with your work? No problem! Instead, get focused about the potential in this changed situation: you're building a strong relationship with your immediate superior – and that's certain to have positive benefits down the road. Your friend can't make dinner, brilliant! You have an opportunity to go for a run or catch up on your favourite TV show or the book you're reading.

2. DETAIL YOUR PLAN B

If, like me, you're a stickler for Plan A, you may feel unsettled when something forces you to change course. If that's the case, it can be really helpful to have a well-thought-out Plan B. Let's say you get stuck in traffic and are going to be late for work; perhaps you'll even miss your first meeting. While you're waiting to get moving again, plan out exactly how an alternative day might look and make the necessary calls and rearrangements as soon as you can. Your day isn't quite the one you were expecting, but with a new plan in place, it's entirely manageable.

3. KEEP IT IN PERSPECTIVE

Traffic detours, a colleague who's late for a meeting, a child who refuses to put on his shoes – irritating as these things might be, in life's bigger picture they probably aren't even episodes you'll remember for more than one day, never mind in the long term. No matter how hard it seems, try your best to recognize that these little changes to your plans aren't usually worth a large amount of stress, and strive to redirect your attention to the big picture whenever you find them irritating you.

4. STAY THANKFUL

In addition to keeping life's annoying little curveballs in perspective, it's also helpful to find hidden reasons to be thankful for them. Yes, you're going to be late for work because of the traffic, but you get to enjoy your audio book for a little while longer; your toddler won't wear shoes, but he's got two healthy, working feet to walk on. Every little irritation in life is an opportunity to find something to be grateful for.

reminder!
POSITIVELY PRESENT PRINCIPLE #5

Adopt an attitude of gratitude for all the little changes that you encounter day by day to keep you from comparing your life unfavourably to the lives of those around you. When you see the reasons to be thankful for small changes, there's no need to covet someone else's situation.

5. RELINQUISH CONTROL

Day-to-day upsets are great reminders that we're not as in control of our lives as we'd like to think. Instead of trying to combat the surprises coming your way and getting stressed, actively choose to let go of control. Clench your fists together and then open your hands, pointing your palms to the sky. Imagine, as you unfurl your fists, that you're letting go of your need to hold the reins of your life. As you do so, you're gaining an acceptance of whatever is happening right now.

CONQUERING YOUR FEAR *of change*

t's perfectly natural to be afraid of change. After all, if something works already, why would you want to embrace something new, something that might not work just as well? Fear of change occurs when you learn that something is going to change before it happens, or when you make your own decision to change something in your life, but then begin to ruminate on the "what-ifs". As hard as it is to embrace big changes, try to remember that it's more life-limiting to have everything stay the same – so try not to let your fear of change prevent you from taking leaps into the unknown. Only when your feet leave the ground will you have the chance to soar.

I've let my own fear hold me back from making changes I knew in my heart would be best for me, because I was scared of the effects I couldn't predict. But, eventually, lack of change grew stifling. Although I might have felt safe with things as they were, my "safe place" was also one buried deep in negativity. Here are my thoughts on conquering your fear of change and leaping into the glorious blue unknown.

reminder!
POSITIVELY PRESENT PRINCIPLE #2

Be aware of – and willing to shift – your thoughts by considering what it might feel like to move your thinking from a place of fear to a place of excitement. The very act of contemplating excitement might make it easier to embrace change. Negative thinking can become positive with the right shift in mindset.

1. TAKE SMALL STEPS

Starting small can help you take big action. Whether or not your little victories contribute to conquering your big fear of change, a bunch of little successes will help to build your confidence, making you feel stronger and braver in general. Let's say you are going for a promotion to department manager, but are afraid others won't respond to your instructions or requests. To build up your confidence as a manager, before you take on the role, ask someone you don't know well to do a small favour for you. As you gain confidence in the positive ways in which people respond to you (and you'll be surprised how much they will!), you'll become more sure of your ability to handle the consequences of your change.

2. HAVE A PLAN

If you have a plan to facilitate your transition from one stage of your life to another, even when you're frightened about what the outcome might be, you'll have done your best to take charge of the change. For example, if you're leaving a job to travel the world, save the money before you resign; if you're planning to move to a new area, take a long weekend or a week's vacation there before you commit, to get a better feel for the place. Having a step-by-step plan in place can help make big changes seem more manageable, and will allow you to worry less about the future and focus more on the present moment.

3. ALLOW DESIRE TO TRUMP FEAR

The reason you sometimes actively instigate change is because you know it's what you need – so you allow your need for change to overwhelm the fear you have about it. For example, if you really dislike your job but fear what it would be like to accept a new position (new colleagues! new workload! new commute!), focus not on what *could be*, but what *is*: your current unhappiness with your present job. When you pay attention to what's happening now, you'll become more in touch with your desire to change because you'll realize what's *not* working in the present. Fear will still be there, but your passion for change will override it, urging you on to move in a more positive direction.

4. SEEK SAGE ADVICE

You're not the first to make a major change in your life and you certainly won't be the last, so you can benefit by seeking advice from those who have initiated similar changes before, those who have already embraced the fear of change and come

APPLY IT!

see the glass half full

Draw a glass on a sheet of a paper and draw a line through the middle of the glass (if drawing isn't your forte, draw a circle or print out the worksheet for this exercise at danidipirro.com/books/guide). In one half, write all of the reasons why the change you're experiencing is scary. Now, in the other half, challenge yourself to write even more reasons why the change might benefit you, considering how this change might ultimately help you grow as a person and make your life feel more positive.

out on the other side. Ask what prompted them to make a change, how they did it and how it made them feel. Also ask what they might have done differently so you can avoid similar mishaps.

5. DON'T LOOK BACK

How often did your mother say to you as a child, "Look where you're going!" If you keep looking back, you're more likely to trip. Once you've made a decision to initiate a change, keep in the moment, watching your step and always moving forward. The temptation to glance back at what's behind you may be strong, but the more you look over your shoulder at the past, the less time you spend experiencing the positive things in your present and watching the exciting new features of your future unfolding in front of you.

6. FOCUS ON CERTAINTY

When a certain change seems intimidating, try focusing on the constants around you. Will your partner or best friend be with you regardless of what's happening? Will you still have the same job or the same home? The chances are, even during major changes in your life, some things are going to stay the same, at least for a while. Remember that this change, however great it feels now, is in fact just a small piece in the jigsaw of your overall life. Be grateful for the current constants in your life, and allow them to ground you when change seems overwhelming.

LOOK WHERE YOU'RE GOING

THIS WAY!

NOT WHERE YOU'VE BEEN

BREAKING *bad habits*

We all have 'em and we all hate 'em – bad habits. I've had quite a few in my life – drinking, smoking, partying, negative thinking, to name a few – and it's been quite a feat to let them go. In some cases, it took years to do so. However, for every bad habit I've broken, I've created a space in my life for a new, positive behaviour instead. And although I still have a few habits I'd be better off without, I know that with the right mindset and the right tactics I have the power to triumph over them.

Of course, some bad habits – such as nail-biting or spending just a little more than we should – are small and manageable. Others, though, are uncontrollable demons – such as alcohol or drug abuse, or eating disorders. These can become so much part of our lives that even though we know we need to let them go, doing so seems impossible, intimidating or downright terrifying. Some habits become so much a part of our lives that, despite them being negative, we are afraid to live *without* them.

It's important to recognize that a truly bad habit – one you know you should let go of as soon as you can – is likely to have negative repercussions in other areas of your life and on your overall wellbeing. For example, it may harm your relationships, negatively affect your job or college work, make you feel guilty, ashamed or depressed, cause you physical or emotional harm, get you into trouble (with loved ones or even with the law), and cause others to become seriously worried about you.

Even the lesser bad habits can cause negativity to trickle into your life. For example, I really wish I didn't drink so many energy drinks. I know they aren't good for me as they're filled with processed products. I'd be much better off with natural sources of energy – such as green tea – and I know it, but part of me wants that shiny, silver, expensive can of energy even though I know it's not what my body needs.

WHEN THE SEA IS ROUGH, keep swimming

Before you read my tips for starting to let go of your bad habits, have a think about how you live and make a list of the habits – both big and small – that aren't doing you any good. Be honest and firm with yourself; don't try to excuse away anything you know in your heart is not good for you (the fact that I don't drink coffee is *not* an excuse to drink all those energy drinks). Bad habits always catch up with you – and the sooner you rid your life of them (or at least reduce their presence), the sooner you can start living more positively in each present moment.

It's no easy thing to break the habit of a lifetime, but when you get rid of something causing negativity in your life, the sense of achievement is one of the most rewarding things you can experience. I might still have some bad habits to tackle, but when I can look back and say, "Wow. I haven't had an alcoholic drink in over *four* years" or "I can't even remember the last time I smoked a cigarette!", it's a truly amazing feeling. Here are some tips to help you bring positive change into your life.

1. COMMIT TO QUIT

If you want to kick a bad habit, it's important to commit yourself fully to doing so. This seems obvious, but people often say, "Yeah, I want to quit that ..." but don't *really* mean it. If you really want to stop, you have to commit mind, body and soul. Sometimes it takes getting to a really low point to make that commitment, but you can miss out on a whole heap of negativity if you can commit before you get there. (When it comes to my energy drink problem, one of the reasons I haven't broken that habit is because of this point right here. Although I say I want to stop drinking those fizzy gems, deep down I'm not ready to let them go. In order to commit yourself fully to breaking a bad habit, you have to really, really *want* to do it.)

2. ASK OTHERS TO HOLD YOU ACCOUNTABLE

It's one thing to tell yourself you're going to break a habit, but it's quite another to share that fact with others. Once you share your intentions with someone else, they can help hold you accountable for staying on track. With someone keeping an eye on your progress and asking you every now and then how you're doing, you're more likely to stick with it. For additional motivation, consider starting a blog to track your progress (and potentially find others who are striving to break the same bad habit). That's what I did when I started PositivelyPresent.com (see page 207), and it was an amazing way to hold myself accountable for breaking my negative thinking patterns.

3. SURROUND YOURSELF WITH HEALTHINESS

When you're working on point 2, it really helps to have healthy, positive people in your life. If the people around you also have your bad habit, or aren't committed to being free from bad habits themselves, they won't be able to help you. If you want to succeed, you may have to avoid people who bring you down (even if it's just until you're habit-free). In addition, try the best you can to keep yourself away from temptation; try not to put yourself in situations where you're likely to give up. For example, if you're trying to stop drinking, don't go to a bar. If you don't want to smoke, go to places that ban smoking.

reminder!
POSITIVELY PRESENT PRINCIPLE #3

Remove negativity whenever possible by putting yourself in positive situations and surrounding yourself with healthy, positive people. This can help when you're attempting to break a bad habit. Positive people and environments almost always push your mind – and your actions! – in a more positive direction.

4. KICK ONE HABIT AT A TIME

Did you make a New Year resolution list? How many of the bad habits on it did you manage to break? We often find New Year resolutions hard to stick to because we're trying to do too much at once. By all means have more than one goal, but focus on breaking only one bad habit at a time. As with multi-tasking, it might seem like a good idea to quit everything at once, but you can commit more completely to overcoming a bad habit if you focus on one issue at a time.

5. SUBSTITUTE A BETTER BEHAVIOUR

Breaking a habit can feel like you're losing a part of yourself, which is why you need to fill the gap quickly with something more positive. Take a close look at the patterns surrounding your bad habit (where do you do it? with whom? why?) and then think of an alternate, healthier behaviour to use as a substitute. For example, if you're trying to quit smoking, but you know you always want to smoke when you're in the car, suck a lollipop or a liquorice stick while driving instead.

6. KEEP TRACK OF YOUR EMOTIONAL STATE

Breaking a habit – especially one that's deeply entrenched in you, or that is a physical addiction – is extremely hard work. It's emotionally draining. Keep an eye on your emotional state and if kicking the habit seems overwhelming, cut yourself some slack and enlist the help of those around you for inspiration, support and encouragement. You don't have to do it all on your own. If you struggle to find people who can keep you in a positive emotional state, consider seeking the help of a licensed professional, particularly one who specializes in the area in which you need help.

7. REWARD YOUR PROGRESS

Most of us do well when we're rewarded for our positive progress, so it's often helpful to offer yourself little rewards as a source of motivation. For example, if you're trying to stop biting your nails, treat yourself to a manicure after you've been bite-free for a week.

APPLY IT!
pinpoint your triggers

One of the best ways to avoid returning to a bad habit is to know exactly when you feel the need to engage in it. Consider which places, situations and emotional states tend to trigger your habit. Do you associate certain people with it? Knowing when and where you're most likely to indulge your habit can help you avoid (or prepare for) your triggers. Download a worksheet to help you at danidipirro.com/books/guide.

Or, if you're trying to stop eating so many sweets, give yourself a special treat at the end of the week by indulging in a delicious, fresh piece of exotic fruit. Remember: you deserve to be rewarded for your efforts to move your life in a more positive direction. Set small, manageable and preferably timed goals leading you to the ultimate goal of your broken habit, and give yourself a treat every time you reach one. Make sure the treat doesn't lead to temptation, though!

REWARD
YOURSELF
(you deserve it!)

USING CHANGE TO BECOME YOUR *best self*

f you're reading this book, you're probably the kind of person who really wants to make the most of your life, who wants to discover ways to become the best possible version of you. But *wanting* that and actually *doing* it are two very different things. Becoming your best self can be difficult because, although you want to remain true to who you are, you also want to change so you can become a better you. The trick is: you don't need to change your core inner self; instead the aim is to change

what is a "best self"?

Your best self is the version of you that you most like, respect and feel positively about. It's the version of you that showcases your strengths and does the best you can with your weaknesses. Your best self isn't a perfect version of you; it's a version that fills you with positivity and makes it incredibly easy to stay present.

your thought patterns, behaviours and actions so that they are in line with this true inner self. In other words, your best self comes from the way you express your innermost self, not from trying to be someone you are not.

Changing to become your best self enables you to see the world through a more positive lens. Your best self highlights your strengths, enables you to pursue your dreams and improves aspects of your character you'd rather not have. In order to get better acquainted with your best self, sometimes you have only to pay attention, being present with your thoughts and listening closely to what's in your heart. But sometimes (probably most of the time), you'll need to direct your thoughts, actions and attitudes carefully to make sure they follow the best possible path.

You might have heard this quote before: "If you want something you've never had, you have to do something you've never done." If you want to embrace traits you know lie within you but have yet to be uncovered (like bravery, imagination or forgiveness), you often have to change your behaviour, actions or mindset in order to reveal the hidden gems lying beneath. Much of the advice in this chapter so far will help you in this respect: changing your attitude, surrounding yourself with only positive people and breaking your bad habits are all good ways to begin following the path to being the best you can be.

However, the most important way to become your best self is to discover what it is you want more (or less) of in your life. That might sound like a basic task, but it can be a bit of a complex endeavour. Here are some tactics for connecting with the best version of you.

reminder!
POSITIVELY PRESENT PRINCIPLE #1

Open your mind to being positive and present in order to become your best self. An open mind will help you think creatively about how you can make small (or big) changes to your environment, to allow you to become the best version of you. To make this easier, try focusing not on what you'll have to let go of, but on what you're reaching for.

1. DETERMINE WHAT'S IMPORTANT TO YOU

If you want to know what you want more or less of in your life, you need to work out what's really important to you. Imagine an absolutely ideal rest-of-your-life scenario. What do you spend your time doing? Who do you spend your time with? How do you feel when you wake every day in your imagined life? Pay close attention to your thoughts and consider whether or not each is actually *your* thought, or if it's a thought that's influenced by someone else in your life. Is it *you* who wants that big, white wedding or is that your mother's dream? Is it *you* who wants the stressful but lucrative career, or is it just that you feel you must follow in your sister's footsteps? Are three children really *your* heart's desire, or is it your partner who wants the big family? Ensure your answers are true to yourself.

2. IDENTIFY WHAT NEEDS TO CHANGE

Once you've determined the life you actually want, it's time to figure out what areas you need to work on. If you are craving more time to yourself, for example, start by scheduling a night – or even just an hour – a week when you give yourself permission to sit in a room alone or do an activity that is entirely about you. Think of your problem from different angles: perhaps your feeling that you don't have enough time to yourself means you now need the freedom of a place of your own. If that's the case, it could be time to set up a meeting with a financial planner to see if home-buying could become a reality. You might also need to consider what in your present situation is preventing you from becoming the best person you can be. Whatever it is, that's what you need to try to stop doing! See the box opposite for some questions to ask yourself when you are exploring the idea of change – your answers might prove enlightening.

3. GET VERY, VERY SPECIFIC

Now that you've identified what changes would transform your life into one that will allow you to be the best version of you, it's time to consider the precise things you need to alter in order to achieve your end-goals. It's important to be very specific about this. Instead of vaguely thinking, "I need to change my surroundings because I'm unhappy at my job," note several concrete steps you can take, such as reducing the amount of time you spend watching TV after work so that you have more time to spend researching job opportunities. Or, let's say you want to find romance. You might think to yourself, "I should change where I spend my time so I can open up opportunities to meet someone new." Narrow that down to a more specific action, such as signing up for a cooking class one night a week. The more specific you are about the changes you can make, the more likely you'll be to achieve exactly what you're hoping to and become the best version of you!

APPLY IT!
choose a change

Sometimes it's hard to know where to begin when it comes to using change to become the best version of you. Below are some questions to help you think about what you might want to transform in and around you. Even if you're already well aware of how to use change to be your best self, you can benefit from jotting down a few lines in answer to each of these questions. To download the questions in order to answer them on paper, visit: danidipirro.com/books/guide.

- Do you spend your time doing things that are meaningful to you?
- Do you strive to avoid activities that bring negativity into your life?
- Do you engage in activities that challenge you in a positive way?
- Do you spend time with positive people who encourage you?
- Do you strive to positively encourage and inspire others?
- Do you allow yourself to notice – but not dwell on – your flaws?
- Do you take responsibility for your actions and choices?
- Do you honour the commitments you make to yourself?
- Do you value your own needs as much as those of others?
- Do you often express gratitude and love to others?
- Do you admit to others when you've made a mistake?
- Do you strive to forgive those who have wronged you?
- Do you try to speak positively about yourself and about others?
- Do you present yourself honestly and openly to others?
- Do you take care of all your physical, emotional and mental needs?
- Do you feel proud of most of the choices you make?
- Do you seek help or guidance when you're struggling?

CONCLUSION

Hooray! You've read through the entire book (or just skipped right to the end, you sneaky little devil!). You've probably come to see why writing this book has meant so much to me. Those two little words – "positive" and "present" – might seem small on the page, but they have had such an amazingly powerful, soul-refreshing, life-changing impact on me. Focusing my attention on living positively in the present has changed me, and every aspect of my life, for the better. And I hope the information I've learned and shared with you here helps you appreciate the power of choosing to stay positive and present, too.

When I read books that are meant to improve my life, their words of wisdom often stay with me for years, coming back to me when I need them most, prompting me to open the pages again and revisit the turned-down corners, the underlined sentences. My hope is that this book will be like that for you – a place of comfort, a source of insight you can turn to again and again. With the five sections mapping out the main aspects of your life in which you can be more positive and present, I hope it will serve as a guide for the times when you're coping with challenges, whether at home, at work, in relationships, in love or during times of change. I hope you will return to this book for encouragement and motivation.

Living a positively present life isn't easy – sometimes some pretty negative people, situations and thoughts will come your way – but having been through some crazy highs and lows, I can say with certainty that focusing on the present and the positive will only bring more goodness, happiness and inspiration into your life. No matter how difficult life seems, staying positive and present can only improve the circumstances. I hope this book has shown you that being positively present is a choice you can always make!

STAY
positive
STAY
present

52 WAYS
TO BE *positively present*

1 Sit quietly (no phone!) in your favourite spot in your favourite room.

2 Turn off your phone and the TV, and dust one entire room from ceiling to floor.

3 Make a list of all the things happening around you at this very moment.

4 Take a soothing, closed-door bubble bath with relaxing lavender candles.

5 Walk around your neighbourhood, noticing any new signs of nature.

6 Make something with your hands – a painting, a meal, a greeting card.

7 List the things you love about your workplace in this moment.

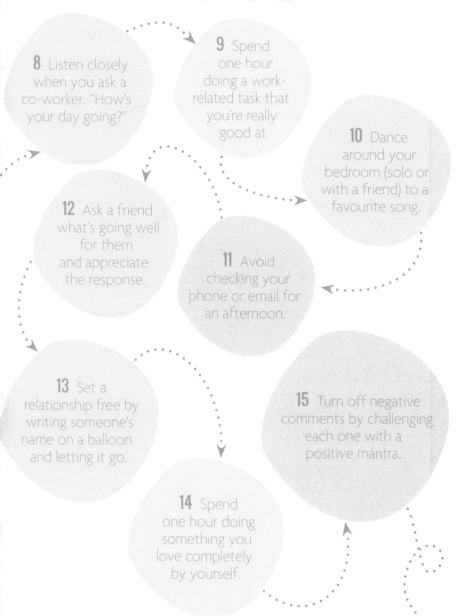

8 Listen closely when you ask a co-worker, "How's your day going?"

9 Spend one hour doing a work-related task that you're really good at.

10 Dance around your bedroom (solo or with a friend) to a favourite song.

12 Ask a friend what's going well for them and appreciate the response.

11 Avoid checking your phone or email for an afternoon.

13 Set a relationship free by writing someone's name on a balloon and letting it go.

15 Turn off negative comments by challenging each one with a positive mantra.

14 Spend one hour doing something you love completely by yourself.

16 Take a new and unexpected route to work or college.

17 Resolve not to compare yourself to anyone for an entire day.

18 Call time-out when you find yourself in a negative conversation and take a walk.

20 Laugh with someone you love by sharing a funny article or watching a comedy together.

19 Look in the mirror and tell yourself ten reasons why you're awesome.

21 Give the person you love a huge hug for absolutely no reason at all.

22 Recreate your first date with your significant other and enjoy every second of reliving it.

23 Tell your loved one something no one else knows about you.

24 Pamper yourself with an at-home spa day.

25 Learn a skill you'll never really need (like juggling, or waltzing or SCUBA diving).

26 Do something childlike (blow bubbles, finger paint, build a fort).

27 Try one thing you think you can't do well (singing, dancing or anything else).

28 Engage your mind with a crossword or sudoku puzzle.

29 Indulge your inner artist by taking a creative course.

30 Watch an animal in the wild and observe its habits and instincts.

32 Stretch for a full five minutes when you wake up in the morning.

31 Give yourself a face and head massage (or trade foot massages with a loved one).

33 Take a "mental health day" and do "sick" things (watch movies in bed, sip soup and so on).

34 Prepare a meal completely from scratch (even if you don't love to cook).

35 Go on a day trip to a town or neighbourhood you've never seen before.

36 Spend time with a dog or cat and note how they stay completely present.

37 Look up to the sky and describe (or draw) how it looks.

38 Eat your favourite food as slowly as possible, being mindful of each bite.

39 Focus on your breathing patterns for a full minute.

40 Photograph your favourite possession, person, pet or place from various angles.

41 Volunteer at a local charity and focus only on what's happening there.

42 Look closely at, and take note of, the details of a plant or flower.

44 Pay close attention to the seasons and how they change.

43 Host a party for those you love most, enjoying it without worrying about the dishes.

45 Listen to your favourite song on repeat, paying attention to why you love it.

46 Start a new project doing something you've never tried before.

47 Take a look around the room you're in, noticing the various colours and textures.

48 Introduce yourself to someone new and ask thought-provoking questions, such as, "What's your clearest memory?"

49 Ask yourself, "What do I love most about this moment?"

51 Tell someone all the reasons why you love them.

50 Call someone you love, who you haven't spoken to in a while, for a nice chat.

52 Smile at every person you see — even if you don't feel like smiling.

FURTHER READING

I absolutely love to read and have learned so much from books. Here are some of the books that have inspired me to live a more positive, more present life.

David Brooks, *The Social Animal*
Augusten Burroughs, *This Is How*
Richard Carlson, *Don't Sweat the Small Stuff*
Shirzad Chamine, *Positive Intelligence*
Gary Chapman, *The Five Love Languages*
Deepak Chopra, Debbie Ford and Marianne Williamson, *The Shadow Effect*
Lori Deschene, *Tiny Buddha*
Barbara Fredrickson, *Positivity*
Christ Guillebeau, *The Happiness of Pursuit*
Jonathan Haidt, *The Happiness Hypothesis*
Susan Jeffers, *Feel the Fear and Do It Anyway*
Anne Katherine, *Boundaries*
Byron Katie, *Loving What Is*
Danielle LaPorte, *The Fire Starter Sessions*
François Lelord, *Hector and the Search for Happiness*

Lee Lipsenthal, *Enjoy Every Sandwich*
Lucy MacDonald, *You Can Be an Optimist*
Daniel A Miller, *Losing Control, Finding Serenity*
Steve Nobel, *The Enlightenment of Work*
Gretchen Rubin, *The Happiness Project*
Don Miguel Ruiz, *The Four Agreements*
MJ Ryan, *The Happiness Makeover*
Karen Salmansohn, *How to Be Happy, Dammit*
Martin EP Seligman, *Learned Optimism*
Susan Shapiro, *Lighting Up*
Sarah Silverton, *The Mindfulness Breakthrough*
Alexandra Stoddard, *Choosing Happiness*
Eckhart Tolle, *The Power of Now*
Karen Whitelaw-Smith, *The Butterfly Experience*

ACKNOWLEDGMENTS

When I was a little girl, my bedroom was filled with books and notebooks and piles of pretty pens. I dreamed of someday publishing a book, of being a real writer. Now here I am – a grown up! – and I'm so incredibly grateful to all those who, directly or indirectly, helped to make my dream a reality.

First and foremost, I must thank my parents and my sister, who have always supported me. Without my parents – two incredibly smart, inspiring and, in some ways, polar opposite individuals – I wouldn't be the person I've become, the person I needed to be to write this book. Mom, thank you for always staying positive (even through those awful teenage years) and for showing me the many benefits of adjusting my attitude. I love you to the sky and back. Dad, thank you for giving me the gift of writing and showing me what it means to be a truly devoted reader. Your love of the written word – and of me! – will be for ever a part of who I am.

To those who have been positive, encouraging supporters – Stephanie Battista, Blair Todd, Dani Ames, Abbey Jacobson, Wade Buckland, Coral Byroad Smith – thank you. I'll be forever grateful for the advice, encouragement and love you shared with me as I worked to transform my life into a place where I could be both positive and present.

A huge thank you to those at Watkins Publishing – Kelly Thompson, John Tintera, Judy Barratt, Fiona Robertson and Georgie Hewitt, in particular – who worked closely with me to create this book, recognizing its potential immediately and dedicating so much time and attention to making it the absolute best it could be. It has been a joy to work with you, and I'm so looking forward to embarking on future projects together.

To all of those who have read PositivelyPresent.com for years: thank you, thank you, thank you! Your support and encouragement make it so easy for me to love what I do. The positivity and love I have felt from you, Positively Present readers, has been one of the driving forces in creating this book and for that I will always be thankful.

ABOUT THE AUTHOR

Dani DiPirro is an author, blogger and designer living in a suburb of Washington, DC. In 2009, she launched the website PositivelyPresent.com with the intention of sharing her insights about living a positive and present life (something that didn't always come easily to her!). Anything and everything focused on positive personal development has a home on Positively Present (see opposite).

In addition to writing *The Positively Present Guide to Life*, Dani is also the author of *Stay Positive: Daily Reminders from Positively Present* and a variety of e-books on specific topics such as self-love, holiday planning, penny-pinching and organization.

While expanding her career as an author and blogger, Dani also began learning about graphic design and illustration. She has since launched a design studio, Twenty3, in which she creates downloadable content on Etsy and designs products for Society 6, and works with individuals and businesses to create modern, uplifting illustrations and designs.

When she's not designing, blogging or writing, Dani can be found with her head in a book, creating inspirational content on Instagram (@positivelypresent), pinning like crazy on Pinterest or playing with her Morkie pup, Barkley.

For more about Dani, visit: DaniDiPirro.com

ABOUT POSITIVELYPRESENT.COM

Someone once said, "If you realized how powerful your thoughts are, you would never think a negative thought." Positively Present is that quote come to life online. In 2009, Dani DiPirro launched the site, focusing on providing readers with practical advice and personal insights about living positively in the present moment. Since then the site has grown considerably and continues to impact the lives of people around the world.

Working hard to embrace the idea of "living happily ever after now," Dani uses Positively Present to focus on finding the positive and embracing the present in her life — and, while doing that, she shares her experiences and real-life wisdom with her readers.

Living a positively present life means staying in the moment while focusing on the positive in every situation, which can often be difficult when facing the pressures and challenges of everyday life (not to mention the particularly tough times of loss, stress or heartache!). Positively Present was created to help Dani and her readers make the most of their moments (even the difficult ones), and the site features insights, inspiration and personal experiences from Dani to uplift and motivate readers.

The website is filled with articles, interviews and resources for creating a positively present life. You'll find tips for being more positive (even when it's hard!), advice for living in the present moment, insights on how to cope with negativity and inspiring, uplifting illustrations. Positively Present is updated twice a week with a new article featured on Monday and a weekly round-up of positive quotes, links, music and resources every Friday. The Positively Present archives include over five years of content sorted by category, and Dani also offers some free printable downloads for her readers.

To learn more about Positively Present, visit: PositivelyPresent.com

WATKINS

Sharing Wisdom Since
1893

The story of Watkins Publishing dates back to March 1893, when John M. Watkins, a scholar of esotericism, overheard his friend and teacher Madame Blavatsky lamenting the fact that there was nowhere in London to buy books on mysticism, occultism or metaphysics. At that moment Watkins was born, soon to become the home of many of the leading lights of spiritual literature, including Carl Jung, Rudolf Steiner, Alice Bailey and Chögyam Trungpa.

Today our passion for vigorous questioning is still resolute. With over 350 titles on our list, Watkins Publishing reflects the development of spiritual thinking and new science over the past 120 years. We remain at the cutting edge, committed to publishing books that change lives.

DISCOVER MORE ...

Read our blog

Watch and listen to
our authors in action

Sign up to
our mailing list

JOIN IN THE CONVERSATION

WatkinsPublishing   @watkinswisdom

WatkinsPublishingLtd   +watkinspublishing1893

Our books celebrate conscious, passionate, wise and happy living.
Be part of the community by visiting

www.watkinspublishing.com